Vote Communist

Vote Democrat

Philip Clark

VOTE COMMUNIST VOTE DEMOCRAT
By Philip Clark
Printed in the United States of America
ISBN 1523253312
ISBN 13: 9781523253319

Table of Contents

Introduction and Reason

THE REASON FOR writing this book is very simple; I love my country, and I fear for it. I believe America is a covenant nation under the hand of Jesus Christ. However, we are facing a real and grave political war for the right to liberty.

There are two Political Religions in this world. One is of Man desiring to control the world by the government of Communism. The other Political Religion is the government of God. His purpose is not to control but to offer peace and eternal life.

So many great men have tried to help us understand just what it means to be blessed to live in the U.S.A. and the freedom it offers. Ronald Reagan warned us not to take it for granted when he said: "Freedom is a fragile thing and is never more than one generation away from extinction. It is not ours by inheritance; it must be fought for and constantly defended by each generation, for it comes only once to a people. Those who have known freedom and then lost it have never known it again." (Reagan, 1967, n.p.)

Historians state more often than not that enemies will destroy nations from within, rather than from foreign countries. That is what is happening to America this day. This day our Constitution, American values, family, and America's love of God is being devastated by our very own countrymen. Many of today's voters are ill-informed of what is taking place.

So much has been given to this nation. Why would anyone want to destroy our Constitution, our Christian religion, and our family values?

To find the answer to these questions, I decided to conduct a wide-reaching search to try to find answers for what is causing our country to be supporting communism over freedom? The problem of knowing the truth is that you have the responsibility to share that knowledge.

Researching to write this book opened up an unexpected door to the real concerns we are facing.

Those concerns are the very reason for sharing this book. I now have a responsibility of opening this truth to the people of this nation. Moreover, I hope the reader will feel that same responsibility to tell the truth about the plights facing America. All American citizens have the same responsibility of sharing the facts with our loved ones, with the citizens of our land. If we do not reach out and educate each other, we will become that one generation away that lost freedom.

This book presents evidence to wake up the voter and reminds us what we need to do so we do not become that generation that loses our inheritance. We must be the generation willing to fight for and defend our love of country and our love of LIBERTY.

The ball is now in our court. The question is what are we going to do with this new knowledge, this new responsibility? America is counting on us to do our part to ensure and protect our Founding Fathers Declaration of Independence and our Constitution; A nation built upon the "Laws of Nature and Nature's God." America a land offering every opportunity for "Life, Liberty, and the Pursuit of Happiness".

Good Luck with this entrusted responsibility while remembering, United we stand divided we fall. Will we now stand up for freedom? America is the world's best hope. If we fail, we may never know freedom again.

Philip Clark
www.america1st.us

Communism
SLAVERY or LIBERTY?

Communism: the power of government to control and direct man's Free Agency and Liberties.

(PHIL CLARK)

America Living in Trepidation (Fearful - Uncertainty)

As AMERICA IS preparing for its upcoming presidential election, a cloud of uncertainty is hanging over the country. A dark shadow brought on by an overwhelming majority of citizens believing America is moving in the wrong direction. Many Americans have concerns over the security of this nation; concerns over increasing racial tension, and concerns over the declining, and breaking down of family values. America is witnessing a deterioration of the Constitution, their personal liberties, and their religious principles brought on by an overextending authority by the President of the United States through executive orders. America is witnessing the Supreme Court manipulating the Constitution for social reasons versus upholding the original intent.

Those most priceless values of the Constitution were designed to maintain and protect the "Laws of Nature and Nature's God," the very principles representing the true God in establishing the "Spirit of America." Today's voters are fed up and even angry in the way their two political parties are failing to ensure their future opportunities for "Life, Liberty, and the Pursuit of Happiness."

Observing what is taking place by our elected Congressional officials, we are witnessing their absence in protecting our country's freedom. Next we see a Supreme Court system perverting our Constitution. Do we not have the right to ask:

"WHAT IS HAPPENING? JUST WHO ARE WE TODAY, WHERE ARE WE GOING AS A NATION, AND WHAT HAS HAPPENED TO OUR HERITAGE AS A NATION, ARE WE STIRRING UPON SLAVERY OR LIBERTY?

It appears we have elected a President who wants to and is "TRANSFORMING AMERICA". As a result of his transformation, America is in a downfall as a worldwide political influence (70% of citizens believe America is at its weakest leadership position in modern history). Transformation failures are increasing poverty, decreasing job opportunities, lowering of family income, increasing racial division, authorizing unlawful acts of immigration, bringing about the very threat of national instability, and loss of Liberty.

Members of Congress have failed to safeguard an expected Balance of Powers between the three branches of government designed with precise purpose as intended by our Founding Fathers. Our elected officials have become feeble minded and weak while demonstrating corrupt moral values resulting in creating a political trepidation filled with concerns of uncertainty for our country.

The culmination of this political alarm has brought about a splintering of Religious Political ideologies. It has brought the fear of what today's government fraudulently represents and the misgivings in Congress in administering the Constitution.

Political Religious doctrines go by many different names and positions. Political names include conservatives, liberals, progressives, leftists, right-leaning, socialists, libertarian, Atheist, Democrats, and Republicans. Examples of organizational names include global warming, same-sex-attraction, and religious followers of Islam or Christian/Judeo beliefs. Each Religious Political ideology consists of a range of varying sets of principles. Each is trying to tell the world his or her particular Political Religious ideology is the one best designed to bring about contentment and personal fulfillment for all humanity during life on this earth.

These concepts may seem somewhat complicated when viewed from the top of the political surface. However, when one dives below the surface with a sincere desire to seek genuine understanding, it is possible to learn there are only two Political Religious ideologies that exist in the world; Ideologies based on Man's way of thinking and belief system founded on their philosophies, and their Political Religion. Man's Political Religious purpose is designed to gain power over its citizens by controlling their LIBERTIES while offering a variation of restricted "freedoms" (Communism).

The ensuing Political Religion is God's government, the opposition to the first. It is designed to yield humanity both liberty and freedom known, as free **agency**. Just stated, the only valid forms of government and Political Religion upon earth are Man's control government (Communism) versus God's government yielding Liberty.

AGENCY of MAN

What is the meaning of the word "AGENCY"? Agency is the mental, intellectual, and spiritual capability to make decisions freely; it is **true Liberty** the **free will of man.** Agency is the ability to choose or reason what is moral or immoral, and not under the control of some other person or some power. Agency is the most valuable quality or attributes a man can possess. It is the right to make independent choices and to choose one's course of life without compulsion. Communism's primary goal is to control man's agency the ability to redirect intellectually and spiritually the way man independently comes to moral/spiritual decisions.

Agency is Liberty the **SPIRIT OF MAN; THE FREE WILL** of Man. Communism must control man's free will to control his desires for liberty to turn him into a mechanical robot. Overcoming man's spiritual, mental, and emotional process of behaving is communism's most decisive

3

religious goal. Once a government is capable of destroying or restraining the free will of man, the government gains total coercion of the physical and intellectual capabilities of man.

China, Iran, and North Korea are examples of coercion government. If their citizens do not follow and conform to their ideas and demands to government rules, lifestyle, and political-religious ideology, severe consequences are paid. They may be imprisoned, tortured, murdered, and absolute loss of Liberty.

Do you believe there is no coercion to conform to a political religion ideology in America? For example, how about when an owner of a bakery wishes not to provide a cake to one who lives an opposing lifestyle may have his business shut down and pay a penalty, or possibly go to jail.

Another example deals with the right to offer prayer on public properties. People argue that prayers should not be allowed in schools and government-run organizations to maintain separation of church and state. However, our Founding Fathers and the Supreme Court often prayed in Congress and Court. A third example deals with individuals being forced to pay taxes for immoral principles, principles that God would not support. In today's America, too often values that were considered right or significant in the past are now being legislated as wrong or disgusting, or repulsive. The list of examples of restricting man's Agency and Liberty in America is growing year by year.

POLITICS and RELIGION

Before moving on, there is a need to provide a definition and clarification of the words Political Religion:

Universally when we think of religion, we think solely of a divine or superhuman power or powers to obey. In Webster's New World Dictionary, 1984 edition, states that it can be defined as "any particular **system of belief**, practice, ethical values, etc. resembling, suggestive of, or likened to such a system of humanism as religion" (p.1134).

Humanism is described as "any system of thought or **action based on non-theistic**, rationalist movement that holds that **man** is capable of **self-fulfillment**, ethical conduct, etc. without recourse to supernatural-ism" (Webster's New World Dictionary, p. 657, 1984).

Putting these two definitions together, we learn that the word religion has two variations of meaning. One is a theology of religion referring to a belief in a **Divine power**. Second is a religion centered on a system of humanism or **"non-theistic** system" or solely stated the way **man desires** to live life. In closing, the meaning of religion is directly based on the philosophical, political, economic, and moral values of a person's way of thinking, belief, and lifestyle. Faith does not require a superhuman or divine source", only one's individual beliefs or preference in life.

Quite often we are in the habit of pigeonholing Religion by limiting or restricting its usage. We must not overlook its full and profound mean-ings, its actions, and its values. To do so, we are failing to recognize and accept its important academic and acquired values. Today that is what is happening to the meaning of Religion, pigeonholed by the non-theists.

Every person in this world has some form or lifestyle of religion they live by, and they do so either consciously or subconsciously. A person who does not believe in a divine God still has a non-divine religion they live by just as much as a person who believes in God. Even the United States Supreme Court in 2005 has stated that atheism, which claims not to be reli-gion, is a non-divine religion or organization so stated as follows:

"The Supreme Court case of James J. Kaufman, v. Gary R. McCaughtry et al. United States Court of Appeals for the Seventh Circuit No. 04-1914 (19 August 2005). The 7th Circuit Court of Appeals declared in 2005 that atheism is a religion for the purposes of protection under the Establishment Clause.

"Again in the case of Wallace vs. Jaffree, the Supreme Court, 472 U.S. 38 (1985) said:

"At one time it was thought that this right (referring to the right to choose one's own creed) merely prescribed the preference of one Christian sect over another, but would not require equal respect for the conscience of the infidel, the atheist, or the adherent of a non-Christian faith such as Islam or Judaism. But when the underlying principle has been examined in the crucible of litigation, the Court has unambiguously concluded that the individual **freedom of conscience** protected by the First Amendment embraces the right to select any religious faith or none at all."

In essence, the Supreme Court has said that it was thought the right to choose a creed (religion) merely prescribed the preference of Christianity. That it did not offer equal respect for the conscience of an atheist or non-Christian faith. However, under the crucible of litigation, atheism (non-Christian) conclusively has the same rights.

Individual freedoms must determinedly be protected as the rights of any religious faith or none at all. Atheism is afforded the same consideration as Christianity under the first amendment and AS A FAITH is respected as an establishment (religion) entitled to the same free exercise of worship equal in practice to Christianity.

Faith does not require the presence of a divine or theological concept but is determined by one's **conscious beliefs**. The Supreme Court, in essence, states: Religion is any system of thought or **action based on one's theistic or non-theistic conscious.**

What is one's conscience? The Webster's Dictionary defines conscience as "having a feeling or knowledge. Aware of oneself as a thinking being; knowing what one is doing and why." (Webster's Dictionary 1984 p. 296.)

Conscience is the mental and physical, **religious lifestyle**, beliefs, actions, and passion the individual lives by each day. Those who live a non-theistic religious life honor their religion but do not want to admit they are religious in a rational way while opposing a religion of a supreme being.

There are those who say they are Christians, but when viewing their actual works, we understand that they are pretentious Christians, wolves in sheep's clothing. They say one thing but live by opposing standards.

When we say the Political Religious philosophy of man we are referring to (but not limited to):

Atheism	Evolutionism	Pantheism,
P rogressivism	Liberalism	Socialism
Islamism	Communism	Global Warming
Democrat	Republican	Pornography
Federal Welfare	Same-sex	One World Gov.

Although the world does not associate with the above-listed categories as being a real form of Political Religion, it is precisely what each one emulates. Each Political Religion is driving a particular set of beliefs, a lifestyle, or philosophy that man advocates in following, teaching, and living. Their Political Religion is their ruling energy that drives their shared passion, their everyday life actions, and their spiritual progression.

Religion even exists in a natural, non-political position as one who spends his life sitting in front of a TV drinking beer and watching Sunday NFL football games; also paying no thought or respects to the divine authority of this world. The god they worship is their beer and football.

As you read, please keep an open mind. Understand that any belief, action, or passion directing a person's lifestyle away from a Christian/ Judeo guided faith, is a religion of Man's god and Man's laws versus a Divine God. The Bible time and again refers to this action as the "worshipping of false idols". An idol can be any material or non-material object, belief in, or passion for one's life that counters the belief in the divine authority of Jesus Christ the Creator of this Earth.

POLITICAL RELIGION

What is the meaning of the words Political Religion and how do they relate one to another or do they belong together?

When reviewing the meaning, purpose, and actions of Political Religion, we recognize there are many different components. However, they all belong in one of two ideologies or philosophical camps. The Religion of Man or the Religion of Jesus Christ, the God, and creator of the earth.

The definition of the word Political means: "of or concerned with the government having a defined government organization." The definition of the word Government is exercising authority over a state, organization, institution, direction control: rule; management." The government is a system of ruling or controlling. (Webster's Dictionary, 1984, P584).

The keywords are: having a defined organization; exercise of a ruling authority over an organization or institution.

Both a physical government of Man and a Moral government of God share the same organizational structure. Both have members (citizens) of the institution, both have leadership positions (President/Bishop), both have meeting locations (Capital buildings/Church buildings), and both follow written guidelines (Constitution/Bible). Therefore, the words Political and Religion are both interchangeable as both consist of the same related and similar structures, objectives and purpose in directing and guiding man to a result. The main difference is Man uses his power to control liberty and agency whereas Christ does not use His power to limit man's freedom, agency, or man's individual liberties.

It is so unfortunate and sad in today's society that people and organizations continue to repeat and live by the misunderstood phrase "separation of church and state." Meaning they believe it is not only wrong but anti-American, and unconstitutional for one to combine state and church or in other words to allow principles of religious thoughts and morals intermixed with government values and activities.

It is because of their strong Political Religion of Man's position that they fail to understand that politics, government, and religion are interchangeable; they are similar in direction and purpose.

The overwhelming majority of the world and the members of the Political Religion of Man are so caught up in their day to day life they are not able to see the trees in the forest. Blinded by their Religious assessment, they are not able to envision their unique role in the **eternal perspective of life** and their relationship to God, their Father. A price to pay they will one day greatly regret.

It is anti-American and unconstitutional **only** when the free exchange of religious values are not allowed to intermix with the government for two reasons. The first reason is that this nation is a Christian Nation politically created by, personally observed by, and politically overseen by Christ's respective Political direction. Our Founding Fathers have a multitude of times testified that God's hand reached out as our protector during the Revolutionary War, His hand was upon the creation of our Constitution. Christ is America's Political creator, mentor, leader, and personal founder.

The second point is that Political Religious beliefs are an accurate reflection of a person's moral character. Therefore, Politics is a man's moral compass to the way he lives his life. A person's moral character is accountable to both Man's laws and God's laws. Man's laws are in existence only during man's duration while on earth. However, God's laws are in existence and force from birth throughout life on earth, during man's expanded life after earth, and throughout all of the man's eternality.

Once we understand the correct meaning of the words Religion, Humanism, Politics, and government we can come to an honest conclusion. Yes, Politics and Religion can be classified as one in purpose one and definition. They are interchangeable, and they intertwine with each other. Politics and Religion are logically impossible to separate. Religion is Politics and Politics is Religion of which Jesus Christ is the greatest of all World Political leaders.

COMMUNISM
IDEALISM, MEANING AND PURPOSE.
The pure ideology of communism offers two critical perceptions. First is the right for government to hold political control or ownership of property, industry, and financial wealth within a country and second those

holdings are redistributed throughout the community in an equal means. The hypothesis is there would be no poor, and everyone would be on a uniform base. Each person would have sufficient means necessary to live a happy and productive life.

The problem is due to the human nature of man Communism never has nor ever will work per planned concept. Someone someplace will always want more than others, and will do whatever it takes to gain power, control, and wealth over others to achieve and fulfill his personal desires. Just consider men like Napoleon, Hitler, and Muhammad all desiring to gain power and control of the world. To gain control requires limiting man's liberty.

The fundamental philosophy of communism is a virtuous concept except 100% of the time it ends up as a totalitarian form of government. Perfect examples of communist leadership are men like Hitler, Lenin, Stalin, Mao Zedong, and Muhammad. Examples of nations who live this totalitarian lifestyle are; Cuba, Russia, China, North Korea, and Iran.

In each case, these leaders murdered, imprisoned, stole both material and non-material objects, took possession of property, industry, enslaved citizens, and even forced women into sex trafficking. People living in communist nations are compelled to subsist on a restricted standard of life, financially subdued, existing under the pretexts of limited freedom, personal liberties, and religious rights, a makeup of the rich and the poor with no middle class. Structured servitude over man's liberties.

When we study the history and variations of communism, the government always ends up with people under overall control with continuous power over man. For that reason the meaning and purpose of communism are defined as **the power to control: man's Free Agency of conscious, Individual Freedom, Liberties and Political Religious rights as directed by Government.** Power and control are the end product denying man life as God intended.

The question for us is: Can or will the political, religious forms of communism ever take hold in America? The truth is it has already begun the process through baby steps taking hold in small unnoticed and incremental ways that are referred to as Pillars of Communism, moving forward one Pillar at a time. Sadly that role is currently being subconsciously played out by America's Democratic political Party. YES, America is being led down the road to communism one Pillar at a time with unforeseen consequence by our Democratic Party.

WRAPPING-UP:

1. America's Trepidations: America is reaching a pinnacle point in its history of fear for the uncertainty of its existence of its freedom.
2. The Supreme Court is perverting the Constitution destroying individual God given rights.
3. Congress has become so inept, feebleminded; corrupt, and no longer capable of protecting American values.
4. Politics/Religion: Religion does not require a superhuman or divine source.
5. The Supreme Court supports all faiths both **non-theistic** and theistic as a constitutionally protected right.
6. Politics, government, and religion are interchangeable concepts; they are similar in direction and purpose.
7. All classifications and practice of Political Religions can only belong in one of two ideologies or philosophical camps; the Religion of Man or the Religion of a divine God, Jesus Christ.
8. Religion is Politics and Politics is Religion.
9. Communism: The fundamental philosophy of communism is a benevolent concept except 100% of the time it ends up as a totalitarian form of government.
10. Overcoming man's spiritual, mental, emotional process of behaving is communism's most decisive religious goal.
11. People who live in communist nations are forced to subsist on a restricted standard of life, are financially subdued while existing under the pretexts of limited freedom, personal liberties, and religious rights.

12. Communism: the power to control man's Free Agency of conscious, Individual Freedoms, Liberties and Political Religion rights.
13. Who was the first world Political leader? Jesus Christ as the creator of the earth, designer of American and the Constitution.

—§—

CHAPTER 2

Democratic Party Ties To Communism

*"America's decline under Obama isn't due to mistake or ignorance...It's a **purposeful**, brilliant plan **to destroy capitalism**, American exceptionalism."*

by WAYNE ALLYN ROOT, a former classmate of Obama:

END GOAL of COMMUNISM

COMMUNISM IS A system where all property is public, and the government gives people things according to their needs. The dictionary definition may look something like any economic theory or system based on ownership of all property by the community as a whole, a hypothetical stage of socialism. A third definition given by Webster's online dictionary stated; an example of communism is the governing system in Cuba where the government controls everything and doles out benefits such as money, health care, and food.

Yes, all three definitions are correct but what is the end goal or driving purpose of communism? It is government's power and control of the people. What then are the most important things communism must control to be in the absolute domination of the individual? It is in managing the liberty, freedom, or agency of man. Managing the agency of man is the bottom line, the ending purpose, the intended resolve of communism is to control man's ability to redirect intellectually and spiritually the way man independently comes to moral/spiritual decisions.

Remember agency is the SPIRIT OF MAN; THE FREE WILL of Man. Communism must control man's free will to control his life desires, his spiritual desires, to turn him into a mindless robot. Overcoming man's spiritual, mental, and emotional process of behaving is communism's most decisive religious goal. Once a government is capable of destroying or restraining the free will of man, the government has total control of the physical and intellectual competencies of man.

China, Iran, and North Korea are examples of coercion government. If their citizens do not follow and conform to their ideas and demands to government rules, lifestyle, and political-religious ideology, severe consequences are paid. They may be imprisoned, tortured, or murdered. In America, our court system may coerce one to go against their Religious beliefs. Government organizations may compel parents in the manner of raising a family. Schools may coerce children into accepting the lifestyle they want students to acknowledge such as Evolution over Creation or homosexuality over Marriage of one man and one woman, and even American Exceptionalism and its Constitution.

GOVERNMENT COERCION

How does a government go about gaining control of the people? The most visible means is through the use of totalitarian control as a military or police state used by China, Russia, Cuba, North Korea, and Iran.

Before this can happen government must be in control of two benchmarks: First, they move to weaken and corrupt the laws of the land giving them ruling authority; second, they refuse to recognize freedom of religion and God as the Lawgiver.

Today this is taking place in China, Russia, Iran, Cuba, and North Korea. Each country governs by a <u>ruling authority other than the people,</u> and they do not look to God for their guiding laws.

NOTE: Iran and allied Muslim nations are not God fearing nations but totalitarian forms of government hiding behind the pretense of a pseudo-religion. Additional discussion on Islam will take place in Chapter 4.

Once a man becomes polluted through communist government influence, they no longer have the ability to make sound moral/spiritual decisions. At that point, the government has become a controlling factor of what is moral or what is considered religious. Once this is achieved government operates by forced coercion overwhelming religious government pressure.

Examples of forced coercion are:

1. National health programs
2. Federal educational programs
3. Federal entitlement programs
4. National debt/tax income control
5. National wage control
6. Right of property control
7. Family, Parents, and marriage control
8. Religion/Church control.

Currently, in varying degrees, government controls are being fully implemented in China, Iran, and Russia. Today America is not far behind. Family, property rights and religion is on the verge of being under government control by non-elected federal programs with the influence of local organizations.

Each of the above points of forced coercions is developed and used by the American Democratic Party. Sadly our pitiful GOP leadership falls right along in step with communist policies. A perfect example is when Paul Ryan and Mitch McConnell caved into Communism and gave the Democrats 95% of everything they wanted in the passing of the 2016 budget bill. "Comrade Senate Minority Leader Harry Reid (D-Nev.) called the deal "wonderful" and House Minority Leader Comrade Nancy Pelosi called the budget a "major victory," and no members of her caucus opposed the bill." Read more: (http://www.politico.com/story/2015/10/house-budget-deal-215238#ixzz3v9yt9xg6).

This is one significant reason why America voters believe it makes no difference what their vote stands for when going to the polls in an election year. GOP leadership lacks the courage to support the citizens and the principles of this country.

If a nation's source of authority comes from the people, who are looking to God as the Lawgiver, then how is it possible for communism to gain control of the population in America?

POINT: To gain control of a God fearing America, Communist must destroy the spirit of the nation: the "Spirit of America" consisting of God, Family, and the United States Constitution. Communist leadership must transform the constitution to meet their desired goals, to control business and property rights through government regulations, to diminish Christian political, religious principles through the courts, control the educational system, and lastly totally break down the human family through entitlement programs. In effect, this is the direction and goal of communism to destroy the "Spirit of America"; this is what has taken place in America over the last 65 years.

For Communism to accomplish their goal of One World Order in America, organizations are currently working through the American Democratic Party as their primary source to achieve their objectives. Once America is brought down to their knees, the rest of the world will fall into the hands of a global Communist One World Order in the matter of a very short period. America's destruction stands as the **key** to One-World government.

The reader may be crying out saying how foolish, how ridiculous, how irresponsible and ignorant can a person be. Only a hateful or radical person would be willing to make such an absurd statement. When one becomes nurtured under the false concepts and progressive influences of communism, since the early part of the 20th century, it is understandable how they live by the "boiling frog syndrome."

BOILING FROG SYNDROME

In the allegory of "Boiling the Frog" story, there is an overwhelming assortment of concealed or unforeseen consequences so very right to life, especially in the Political Religious world.

When preparing a live frog for dinner, first start out by placing the frog in a large pot of cool water that is very pleasing to the frog. Then slowly turn up the heat in such a way that the frog never comes to realize what is happening to him. As the water warms up ever so slowly, causing the frog to relax, he starts dozing off in his comfortable environment of the friendly and comfortable numbness of the gentle warm water. In time, the temperature affects the frog in such a way that he starts to drift off to sleep while paying no attention, the frog overwhelmed by the heat that puts him into a stupor or a comatose state while utterly being cooked for dinner.

That is what is precisely happening to the America people today. The Democratic voters have been blindly voting for the Democratic Party ever since the early 1930's and right up to our present day. The Frog (American people), through the help of the Democratic politicians and their loyal voters, is finally reaching the boiling point to be served for dinner to the one-party designs of the Communist/Democratic Party.

Those who vote for the Democratic Party, most assuredly, will cringe at the very suggestion of their party leading America towards communism, and some Democrats will display an attitude of open contempt and disdain. They will say "Come on now we live in America, and that is a ridiculous idea about the Democratic Party and their voters."

We live in a land founded upon the Declaration of Independence and the Constitution based on the principles of "Life, Liberty, and the pursuit of Happiness." Communism is a totalitarian system of government, like China or Iran, with extensive restrictions on freedom of speech, freedom of religion, and the right to property ownership thereby controlled by active regulatory law enforcement". Democrats will continue to say the Democratic Party portrays none of these government influences.

However, that is just what the Democratic Party has been doing with:

1. The institution of liberal non-constitutional judges.
2. Their Marriage/Same-sex courts.
3. Breaking down of the family,
4. Misguided Immigration influence.

5. National Security Agency actions.
6. Attacking First and Second amendments along with Christian beliefs.
7. Environmental Protection Agency is controlling property rights.
8. Redistribution of wealth.
9. Entitlement programs.
10. Taxation for abortion.
11. Affordable Health Care (Obamacare).
12. Secular Education

Moreover, the list does not stop there; it is only a beginning in duplicating and fostering communist political ideology.

It is not meant to imply that it is the Democratic voters' long range envisioned goal to openly "Transform" America into a communist nation. However, it is the actual goal of their **leadership**. Without question, they are intentionally leading America down the road to communism. American style communism, versus Russian or Chinese's strong-arm police action control, is communism through courts and congressional power while discarding the "Laws of Nature", of "Natures God," and the 1ˢᵗ amendment. The very Laws of Nature, which guarantee America's freedom of agency, liberty and religion, being disregarded.

The Democratic Party's real intentions are to act counter to what they falsely proclaim. They want to lead our country in the direction of liberalism, leftist, and or the progressive governmental system of life for the enrichment and well-being of the people. They want to persuade and convince America that their ideology is by far the fairest and most optimal way to guide America. They say they intend to fulfill the utmost human and righteous means of supporting the concept of "Life, Liberty, and the Pursuit of Happiness." Moreover, provides for and guarantees all citizens the greatest opportunity for equal opportunity in life.

First of all, none of their policies should be labeled liberal or progressive but as Communist policies: Communism is the only accurate Politically Correct word that can honestly describe their desires for America.

The following reasons clearly define why the name of the Democratic Party should be the Communist Democratic Party. First the name of Communism. The Democrats proclaim they are Americans who believe in liberal, progressive, or left-leaning government policies. Each of these policies leads to more government control over individual income through redistribution and by taxation, over reaching the rights of individual agency (personal freedom/liberty), while regulating religious expression and personal property rights. Regulation is what America is precisely experiencing today as the result of their "Boiling the Frog" programs for our American citizens through the chivalry of our American Communist Democratic Party.

The second reason the Democratic Party should be called the Communist Democratic Party is due to their religious perspective, which is their anti-God position in denying the right to religious freedom and the right to live one's beliefs as a Christian to follow their God. It is true, many Democrats will say they are Christians. Even the current President of the United States says he is a Christian. However; their political actions show total discontent for Christ. They show disregard for the actual meaning of God's Laws of Marriage. They support homosexuality by court control of indoctrination training through sensitivity programs in our schools, business, and employment.

They also support a communist pseudo-Islam over a true religion of God. Another issue is the enforcement of the controversial Common Core Education program while they refuse to allow public prayer in schools. However, at the same time they are willing to provide special prayer areas for the Islamic students. Also, the manner in which our educational institutions and Child Protective Agency invade and control parents' rights to raise their families. All of which follows right along communist principles and practices. Last, but not least is their removal of God from their party in the 2014 Democratic Party platform. Democrats both consciously and subconsciously desire to replace God's laws with Man's Religious philosophy by refusing to be guided by God.

NOTE: The Laws of God are both universal and eternal. They are the laws that the universe and our world were created and governed by.

Man's laws will last only during this lifetime. When Jesus Christ returns to preside over the earth, His laws will be the only governing laws for each and every nation and all humanity. Please keep in mind there are always consequences for man each and every time man disavows Gods laws.

The third reason for the name of Communist Democratic Party is their deceitful and pathological lies while concealing and withholding their hidden agendas from the America people. To start with, consider their lies, their dishonest positions on Obamacare and Iran policies, a vast hidden tax increase to the middle class and the poor, and their agenda for their illegal immigration decree. All of which place the Democratic Party right next to the way Russia and China govern their people.

If the Democratic Party is not leading America down the road to communism, why do they demand America only accept their ideology of what is right and what is wrong?

For the reader who wants to believe this position, claiming the Democrats are leading America to communism is way off base; let's look at history and how they are stripping us of our liberty.

AMERICAN'S HISTORY of COMMUNISM

As recorded in U.S. history America's first experiment with communism took place in 1620 by the Plymouth Colony's Puritans of the Mayflower compact.

"By painful experience, the Pilgrims learned something that should never be forgotten. Two hundred twenty-seven years before Karl Marx and Friedrich Engels published *The Communist Manifesto,* in 1620, they disembarked from the Mayflower in the New World and established a colony based on communism, **and it did not work.**

"William Bradford was the governor of Plymouth Colony for over 30 years and kept a journal that was eventually published two hundred years after his death: *"Of Plymouth Plantation."* In his journal Bradford talked about the problems associated with living in a communist society:

"The strong, or man of parts, had no more division of victuals & clothes, than he that was weak and not able to do a quarter ye other could; this was thought unjust. As for men's wives to be commanded to do service for other men, as dressing their meat, washing their clothes &, etc. **they deemed it a kind of slavery,** *neither could many husbands well brook it."* (Bolding added). Notice the comparison of communism to slavery. (http://www.jpattitude.com/121122.php: by J.P. Travis).

As indicated the main factors of the Mayflower form of communism was community control of the property and its redistribution of production. As stated by the citizens of Plymouth Colony, their form of government ended in slavery.

Due to the wisdom and Christian beliefs of our Founding Fathers, they created our Declaration of Independence and the United States Constitution. Designed by the "endowment of their Creator", "Laws of Nature of Natures God", and the people, not by or for a ruling class. Who is the Creator and of Natures God as proclaimed in the Declaration of Independence? It is God thereby calling out that our nation is founded on the Religious Political leadership of God our Father, a Christian nation.

Whereas, Communism design is for a ruling authority or class, government by a ruling power. For Communism to control America, they are required to create a new style or form of communism to control property and business. They will allow ownership of goods and companies, but they will control the use and outcome by extensive regulations and taxation. That is how communism in America differs from the typical design of world Communism.

Next in line was George Rapp's socialist community organized as the Harmony Society in Pennsylvania. As a separatist's movement, the followers of Rapp left Germany and in 1804 **"**Rapp was able to secure a large tract of land in Pennsylvania and started his first commune. This first commune, 'Harmonie', (Harmony), Butler County, Pennsylvania, soon grew to a population of about 800 and was highly profitable. At Harmony, the Harmony Society was formally organized on February 15, 1805, and its members contracted to hold all property in common and to submit to spiritual and material leadership by Rapp and associates". The Harmony Society ended in the year of 1906. (https://en.wikipedia.org/wiki/George_Rapp).

Today's "Communist Party USA headquarters location is New York City. For decades, its West Coast newspaper was the *People's World*, and its East Coast newspaper was *The Daily World.* The two papers merged in 1986 into the People's Weekly World. The PWW has since become an online-only publication, called People's World. The party's former theoretical journal, Political Affairs Magazine, is now also published exclusively online, but the party still maintains International Publishers as its publishing house. In June 2014, the Party held its 30th National Convention in Chicago. The party has since officially adopted Marxism-Leninism within its program. In 2014, the new draft of the party constitution declared: "We apply the scientific outlook developed by Marx, Engels, Lenin and others in the context of our American history, culture and traditions." (https://en.wikipedia.org/wiki/Communist_Party_USA).

From its creation in 1919 until today the Communist Party membership has been on a rollercoaster from a high of 200,000 down to 2,000 members. However, the accurate membership number is not and will not be made available to the public. For the Communist to successfully infiltrate, they must hide their identity and intentions.

Since the 20th century, the Communist Party of USA has worked very hard to infiltrate every major social and government organization. Their intentions are to **direct** government policies, <u>educational reforms, church activities</u>, newspapers, and entertainment, and policies.

ROOSEVELT a road to SOCIALISM/COMMUNISM

Franklin Delano Roosevelt was born January 30, 1882, most commonly called by his initials as FDR, passed away on April 12, 1945. As a member of the Democratic Party, while serving as the 32nd President of the United States, he held that position as the longest-serving president for a total of four consecutive terms from March 1933 until his death in April 1945.

FDR was elected at a time of worldwide economic depression, referred to as The Great Depression (1929-39); it was the deepest and longest-lasting economic recession in the history of America. During FDR's presidency, America entered WW II with the invasion of Pearl Harbor (December 7, 1942) until its "V-DAY" ending the war on September 2, 1945.

During the depression upwards of 29% of people were unemployed and about 50% of all banks forced out of business. Because of these economic conditions facing the nation FDR instituted a program known as the "New Deal Coalition." The New Deal Coalition was the alignment of interest groups and voting blocs in the United States that supported the New Deal and voted for Democratic presidential candidates from 1932 until the late 1960s.

With the overreaching effects of the New Deal Coalition, FDR created programs such as the Civilian Conservation Corps (CCC), Civil Works Administration (CWA), and Public Works Administration (PWA). All of which were designed to open employment opportunities in hopes of bringing back economic recovery to America. The Social Security Act created to combat widespread poverty among senior citizens; providing income to retired wage earners from 1935 to the present day.

Unfortunately, world conditions set the stage for one of the longest and bloodiest war started by Hitler. However, even before Hitler's movement for global power Vladimir Lenin was making his power known as the head of the Soviet Union from 1917, until his death in 1922. Lenin _transformed_ Russia into a <u>one-party</u> socialist state; where all land, natural resources, and industry were confiscated and nationalized, ideologically Marxists. Could this also be a transformation design for America by the Democrats?

Like Hitler, Lenin had desires of world power which included America. With Lenin's leadership, the Communist Party of USA became an important spy organization for the Soviet Union. They were successful infiltrating every government department, dealing with the United States internal, national, and worldwide political involvements, infiltrating unions, <u>education systems</u>, and most importantly Congress and the White House.

After the death of Lenin, Joseph Stalin became the leader of the Soviet Union from the mid-1920s until his death in 1953. Holding the post of the General Secretary of the Central Committee of the Communist Party of the Soviet Union, he was effectively the dictator of the state. A bloodthirsty dictator who carried on a most successful spy cell organization in America reaching up to the President, President FDR.

The Freedom of Information Act, created in 1966, also referred to as the FOIA, is a law that gives citizens the right to access information from the federal government. FOIA is the law that keeps citizens aware of their government's business. Because of this act, people are learning about what is taking place in our country.

FOIA evidence is making it possible to know about the actual policies of FDR and informing the citizens of just who was the real FDR, the president of our nation. For a quick digest on FDR read online articles such as http://www.dcdave.com/article5/110211.htm,
http://www.dcdave.com/article5/061203.htm,
http://www.dcdave.com/article5/070113.htm, and
http://newsroom.ucla.edu/topics/nation.

With the Knowledge of such documents, we learn how badly the Soviet Union infiltrated the United States with their various spy cells. At least, on three occasions President Roosevelt was in a face to face conversation with top White House personnel warning him of Russian spies to the point that the Soviets were aware of his policies even before acted on by Roosevelt.

His response was shocking to those who tried to confide in him of the dangers that were taking place. "Roosevelt's attitude toward espionage by the Soviet Communists was permissive (freely allowed, tolerated) in the extreme. Each time Roosevelt had blown off those who were informing him. Spying for the Reds under Roosevelt was virtually risk-free."
(http://www.dcdave.com/article5/110211.htm).

"From Major Jordan's Diaries (a citizen soldier appointed to the post of chief Lend-Lease expediter) we learn that Major Jordon was assigned to work with our Soviet allies to supply them with war materials. He explains in first-hand knowledge how we gave the Soviets the plans and materials to build our Atomic bomb, a cost of materials of over 2006 value of $161,000,000." (http://www.dcdave.com/article5/061203.htm).

Just before Roosevelts' death, Roosevelt and Stalin formulated and negotiated plans to govern the war-torn nations, just as President Obama caved into Iran, FDR caved into Stalin. As Donald Trump might say, "our leaders are stupid." **No, they are just Communists working together.** Stalin walked away with FDR conceding Soviet domination of over half of Europe and with a political advantage over China and Korea. Plus, FDR presented Stalin with all the needed wherewithal to make nuclear weapons. As with Obama and Iran, the question is "what did America gain by negotiating with Stalin"?

Economic historians have investigated and written about the actual failings of FDR's policies during the Great Depression. It is well documented that because of FDR's policies the depression was delayed and extended.

Meg Sullivan posted on August 10, 2004, (http://newsroom.ucla.edu/releases/FDR-s-Policies-Prolonged-Depression-5409 the following).

"Two UCLA economists say they have figured out why the Great Depression dragged on for almost 15 years, and they blame a suspect previously thought to be beyond reproach: President Franklin D. Roosevelt.

"After scrutinizing Roosevelt's record for four years, Harold L. Cole, and Lee E. Ohanian conclude in a new study that New Deal policies signed into law 71 years ago thwarted economic recovery for seven long years.

"Why the Great Depression lasted so long has always been a great mystery. Because we never really knew the reason, we have always worried whether we would have another 10- to 15-year economic slump," said Ohanian, vice chair of UCLA's Department of Economics. "We found that a relapse is not likely unless lawmakers gum up a recovery with ill-conceived stimulus policies."

A second article by the same two professors further explained: Misguided government policies (New Deal Communist stimulus policies) prolonged the Great Depression. (Lee E. Ohanian and Harold L. Cole, February 06, 2009.)

"So what stopped a blockbuster recovery from ever starting? The New Deal. Some New Deal policies certainly benefited the economy by establishing a basic social safety net for Social Security and unemployment benefits, and by stabilizing the financial system through deposit insurance and the Securities Exchange Commission. However, others violated the most basic economic principles by suppressing competition and setting prices and wages in many sectors well above their normal levels. All told, these antimarket policies choked off powerful recovery forces that would have plausibly returned the economy back to trend by the mid-1930s."

Roosevelt's' policies gummed up the recovery because of "ill-conceived stimulus policies" suppressing competition setting price and wage above average levels. Roosevelts' policies replaced capitalism with socialism; exactly what Bush's and Obama's stimulus policies have done to America.

In recapping Roosevelt's role as president, Roosevelts' policies stand out with three new developments in America. First is his introduction of socialism, the starting phase of communism, with his failed employment projects. Second Roosevelt was a communist sympathizer advancing worldwide communism when helping to turn the Soviet Union into a world superpower, placing half of Europe and Korea under Stalin's dictator control. Stalin handled some 50 million murders during his leadership.

Third, Roosevelt's' policies elevated the Democratic Party to 71 years of government control and influence. Policies of socialism as recorded which delayed the depression.

Likewise, Obama's presidency has carried on with Roosevelt pure socialist systems, stymying growth and future development of America. As of 2015, under Obama, America have 50% of citizens receiving some form of social welfare. Big government employment has reached an all-time high; 93 million individuals are either under-employed or unemployed. Obama's policy has created the longest period in America of no growth or the lowest and slowest period of growth. An Obama policy has placed the national debt at an unparallel 19 TRILLION dollars - Obama and Roosevelt all over again.

COMMUNIST GOALS

In 1958, Dr. Cleon Skousen, a former FBI agent, published the book "*The Naked Communist*". Within the book, there is a listing of what is called the "Current Communist Goals." Parts of the book gained so much credence Congress placed it in the Congressional Records and read it on the floor of Congress as follows: (highlighted points added)

Communist Goals (1963) Congressional Record--Appendix, pp. A34-A35 January 10, 1963.

Current Communist Goals EXTENSION OF REMARKS OF HON. A. S. HERLONG, JR. OF FLORIDA IN THE HOUSE OF REPRESENTATIVES

Thursday, January 10, 1963.

"Mr. HERLONG. Mr. Speaker, Mrs. Patricia Nordman of De Land, Fla., is an ardent and articulate opponent of communism, and until recently published the De Land Courier, which she dedicated to the purpose of alerting the public to the dangers of communism in America.

"At Mrs. Nordman's request, I include in the RECORD, under unanimous consent, the following "Current Communist Goals," which she identifies as an excerpt from "The Naked Communist," by Cleon Skousen:"

1. U.S. acceptance of coexistence as the only alternative to atomic war.
2. U.S. willingness to capitulate in preference to engaging in atomic war.
3. **Develop the illusion that total disarmament [by] the United States** would be a demonstration of moral strength.

4. **Permit free trade between all nations regardless of Communist affiliation and regardless of whether or not items could be for war**.
5. Extension of long-term loans to Russia and Soviet satellites.
6. **Provide American aid to all nations regardless of Communist domination**.
7. **Grant recognition of Red China. Admission of Red China to the U.N.**
8. Set up East and West Germany as separate states despite Khrushchev's promise in 1955 to settle the German question by free elections under supervision of the U.N.
9. **Prolong the conferences to ban atomic tests** because the United States has agreed to suspend tests as long as negotiations are in progress.
10. **Allow all Soviet satellites individual representation in the U.N.** (All Soviet countries)
11. **Promote the U.N.** as the only hope for humanity. **Demand that it be set up as a one-world government with its independent armed forces**. (Some Communist leaders believe the world can be taken over easily by the U.N. instead by Moscow.)
12. Resist any attempt to outlaw the Communist Party.
13. Do away with all loyalty oaths.
14. Continue giving Russia access to the U.S. Patent Office.
15. ***Capture one or both of the political parties in the United States***.
16. **Use technical decisions of the courts to weaken basic American institutions** by claiming their activities violate civil rights.
17. **Get control of the schools**. Use them as transmission belts for socialism and current Communist propaganda. Soften the curriculum. **Get control of teachers' associations**.
18. Gain control of all student newspapers.
19. Use student riots to foment public protests against programs or organizations that are under Communist attack.

20. **Infiltrate the press.** Get control of book-review assignments, editorial writing, and policy-making positions.
21. **Gain control of key positions in radio, TV, and motion pictures.**
22. **Continue discrediting American culture** by degrading all forms of artistic expression. An American Communist cell was told to "eliminate all good sculpture from parks and buildings, substitute shapeless, awkward and meaningless forms."
23. Control art critics and directors of art museums. "Our plan is to promote ugliness, repulsive, meaningless art."
24. **Eliminate all laws governing obscenity** by calling them "censorship" and a violation of free speech and free press.
25. **Break down cultural standards of morality by promoting pornography** and obscenity in books, magazines, motion pictures, radio, and TV.
26. **Present homosexuality,** degeneracy and promiscuity as "normal, natural, and healthy."
27. **Infiltrate the churches and replace revealed religion with "social" religion. Discredit the Bible** and emphasize the need for intellectual maturity, which does not need a "religious crutch."
28. **Eliminate prayer or any phase of religious expression in the schools** on the ground that it violates the principle of "separation of church and state."
29. **Discredit the American Constitution** by calling it inadequate, old-fashioned, out of step with modern needs, a hindrance to cooperation between nations on a worldwide basis.
30. **Discredit the American Founding Fathers**. Present them as selfish aristocrats who had no concern for the "common man."
31. **Belittle all forms of American culture and discourage the teaching of American history** on the ground that it was only a minor part of the "big picture."
32. **Support any socialist movement** to give centralized control over any part of the culture--**education, social agencies, welfare programs,** mental health clinics.

33. Eliminate all laws or procedures that interfere with the operation of the Communist apparatus.
34. Eliminate the House Committee on Un-American Activities.
35. Discredit and eventually **dismantle the FBI.**
36. **Infiltrate** and gain control of more **unions**.
37. **Infiltrate** and gain control of all the **largest companies**.
38. Transfer some of the powers of arrest from the police to social agencies. Treat all behavioral problems as psychiatric disorders that no one but psychiatrists can understand [or treat].
39. Dominate the psychiatric profession and use mental health laws as a means of gaining coercive control over those who oppose Communist goals.
40. **Discredit the family as an institution**. Encourage promiscuity and easy divorce.
41. **Emphasize the need to raise children away from the negative influence of parents.** Attribute prejudices, mental blocks and retarding of children to suppressive influence of parents.
42. Create the impression that violence and insurrection are legitimate aspects of the American tradition. That students and special-interest groups should rise and use ["]united force["] to solve economic, political or social problems.
43. Overthrow all colonial governments before native populations are ready for self-government.
44. Internationalize the Panama Canal.
45. Repeal the Connally reservation so the United States cannot prevent the World Court from seizing jurisdiction [over domestic problems. Give the World Court jurisdiction] over nations and individuals alike.

The Connally Reservation does not preclude the Court from assuming jurisdiction; it merely requires American compliance. It already has occurred with the monitoring of the 2012 elections. The American people are beginning to demand a world community presence in this country to stop the systematic abuse of the poor and minorities, so the International Court acts as a perfect refuge for our grievances.

Communist goals reached acceptance in 1958. Today, as we approach the 2016 Presidential election, we recognize a majority of the goals are active today. Especially number 15 to **_capture one or both of the political parties in the United States._** The Communist organization has been successful in controlling the Democratic Party as they continue working on the Republican Party. When reviewing the 45 goals citizens can see many as platform agendas and voting records of the Democratic Party. So far the Communist Party is receiving limited success capturing the Republican Party. However, because of the ignorance of the Republican Party leadership, they have carried on with most of the Democrat's communist goals like welfare and educational programs.

PRESIDENT BILL CLINTON

An article written by J.R. Nyquist of the WorldNetDaily opens some very shocking things about President William Jefferson Clinton the 42nd President of the United States. After reading this story, it is believed Mr. Nyquist offered both sincere and genuine comments on the real character of William Jefferson Clinton. The reader is invited to research this story titled "Why some of us fear Clinton?" (World Net Daily, THURSDAY, JULY 22, 1999, by J.R. Nyquist of the WorldrldNetDaily).

(http://www.cuttingedge.org/news/n1315.cfm). Enclosed is an outline of his main points as follows:

1. Derek Shearer, a possible communist follower, gave a speech at a college in California on overthrowing the dictatorship of the bourgeoisie' in America.
2. To be accomplished by **taking over** members of the Democratic Party.
3. Possible by electing a stealth socialist president.
4. Capitalism made to appear as a bankrupt system.

5. All business to be nationalized by the government.
6. This socialist president possibly elected sometime after 1988.
7. The organization held high hopes for Arkansas governor, Bill Clinton.
8. In December of 1969, Clinton spent three weeks visiting the Kremlin and the KGB.
9. Several Secret Service agents for Clinton wore red Lenin lapel pins.
10. They also carried Chairman Mao's Red Book!
11. Clinton disarmed the military by 50%.
12. Assisted Communist China is attaining first-strike intercontinental ballistic missiles.
13. During the 1996 Re-election campaign, China contributed untold millions of dollars of "campaign contributions" to the Democratic National Committee.
14. Pointed out that Clinton is a secret Illuminist.

CLINTON is more than a COMMUNIST SYMPATHIZER!

For the reader, enclosed are five quotes to support facts that Bill Clinton is a communist supporter:

#1. PRESIDENT CLINTON HANDS CHINA NUCLEAR SECRETS.

"According to Poe, "Federal investigators later concluded that China made off with the 'crown jewels' of our nuclear weapons research under Clinton's open-door policy -- probably including design specifications for suitcase nukes."

"But declassification was not the only means by which President Clinton transferred missile technology and nuclear secrets to the Chinese. He also permitted those secrets to be sold directly to Beijing.

"'We like your president. We want to see him reelected,' former Chinese intelligence Chief General Ji Shengde told Chinagate bag-man Johnny Chung.

"Indeed, Chinese intelligence organized a massive covert operation aimed at tilting the 1996 election Clinton's way.

"In a related move, Clinton in 1997 awarded a 25- to 50-year contract to Hutchinson Whampoa Ltd., a Hong Kong-based shipping firm with ties to Communist China's government and its People's Liberation Army. The contract authorized Hutchinson to control the two major ports on the Panama Canal's Atlantic and Pacific entrances.

"This administration is allowing a scenario to develop where U.S. national security interests could not be protected without confronting the Chinese communists in the Americas. U.S. naval ships will be at the mercy of Chinese-controlled pilots and could even be denied passage through the Panama Canal by Hutchinson, an arm of the People's Liberation Army. In addition, the Chinese Communist Party will gain an intelligence information advantage by controlling this strategic chokepoint. It appears that we have given away the farm without a shot being fired."

Noting the ominous implications of this, Richard Poe observed: "China can now strike U.S. targets easily from their bases in Panama, Vancouver, and the Bahamas." (http://www.discoverthenetworks.org/individualProfile.asp?indid=644).

#2. THE CHINA CONNECTION IS THE REAL SCANDAL

"Now we know why the Democrats were so vicious in their attacks on Senator Fred Thompson (R-TN) and Rep. Dan Burton (R-IN). Theirs were the committees that were closing in on the China connection, the scandal that can bring down the Clinton presidency, the scandal that has made Congressmen start to utter the T-word (treason). A series of front-page news stories in the *New York Times* (May 15, 16, 17) essentially vindicated Thompson's charge that the Chinese Communist Government tried to influence the 1996 U.S. election with campaign contributions.

"Bill Clinton's friend and ubiquitous Democratic fundraiser Johnny Chung told Federal investigators that he funneled nearly $100,000 from the Communist Chinese military to the Democratic campaign in the summer of 1996. The money was handed to Chung by the daughter of the top commander of China's People's Liberation Army, General Liu Huaqing, who was also one of the top five members of the Chinese Communist Party's ruling Politburo." (http://www.eagleforum.org/psr/1998/june98/psrjune98.html).

#3. BILL CLINTON SAYS AMERICANS WILL GET USED TO COMMUNISM

"I can hear Fidel Castro, Hugo Chavez, and Vladimir Lenin telling their people. "In time you'll learn to love Communism… **Obama Care is like the early stages of communism**. Communist ideology is all about equality. "From each according to his ability, to each according to their needs" is a slogan popularized by Karl Marx in 1875." (Bold added).

(Read more at http://godfatherpolitics.com/12723/bill-clinton-says-americans-will-get-use-communism/#BgFeDwt7tU1HXHBD.99).

#4. "CLINTON HAS HELPED MARXISTS AND TERRORISTS AND THEIR "WORLD REVOLUTION" AT EVERY OPPORTUNITY." –U.S. ARMY BRIGADIER GENERAL ALBION KNIGHT, JR. (RET)

"In late December 1969, Bill Clinton crossed the Finnish border into the USSR and boarded a train for Moscow, the center of world atheism and the capital of the Soviet-Marxist state.

" William Jefferson Clinton's pilgrimage to the Soviet Union was the climax of a busy fall semester as a "Rhodes Scholar" at Oxford. It should perhaps be mentioned to those impressed by such presumed status that Rhodes Scholarships are granted to individuals passing ideological muster whose sentiments during the interview process are reflective of **acceptable left-wing views** to the selection committees, and not because of good grades.

"Once in England, Clinton lived up the expectations of his promoters and joined the British Peace Council, which was established by the **British Communist Party**.

"This explains why Chinese Communist agents could obtain sensitive positions within the Federal Government without having to obtain requisite security background checks. This explains how they could steal all our nuclear secrets—and God knows what else—and walk away with impunity, without a peep or protestation from the White House.

"This explains why we are backing the Kosovo Liberation Army—a terrorist gang of drug-**financed Marxist thugs**—and why we are attempting to bomb into submission the socialistic but nationalistic nation which opposes them.

"Yes, this explains a lot of things about Bill Clinton. Clinton has been a left-wing sympathizer (communist) all his life and has appointed openly pro-Communists to his administration, has promoted one Socialist measure after another in the U.S. Congress, has implemented policies calculated to subvert and weaken both the moral and physical defenses of the United States while **doing everything possible to wreck the predominant cultural heritage of this nation**." ("Clinton's Czech-communist connection," Joel A. Ruth, April 30, 1999, WorldNetDaily) (Bold added) (http://www.tldm.org/news2/sellout.htm).

#5. BILL & HILLARY CLINTON LINKED TO MARXIST.
"Back in 1993, I received a 49-page report entitled "Secret: FBI Documents **Link Bill & Hillary Clinton to Marxist-Terrorist Network**," published by the Sunset Research Group of Wichita, Kansas. It was a meticulously documented report showing the connections of the **Clintons to the Institute for Policy Studies, a Marxist think tank** in Washington. Clinton's top economic advisor was Derek Shearer, an IPS operative, and **advocate of Marxist socialism.** Shearer's sister Brooke was also Hillary's traveling companion. The report states: **"In a 1980 book he authored, Shearer confided that he and others were planning to so influence the Democratic Party that a President sharing their Marxist-socialist views could soon be elected."** (Bold added) ("The Gramscian commie in the White House," Dr. Samuel L. Blumenfeld, September 19, 2000, WorldNetDaily).

America, why do we elect people who hold no concerns for the security of our country? People who are more for power, one world order, and money? Support Communist policies?

ILLUMINATI ORGANIZATION

"The Illuminati is a secret organization of the most powerful and influential elite in the world. They go back for centuries and maintain the same bloodlines. They set up the council on foreign relations, the Bilderberg group, and the tri-lateral commission. Those three groups all meet to plan the fate of the world. They consist of international bankers, top government officials, leaders in the energy cartel and media monopoly owners. They have control over the U.N., and UNESCO (United Nation Education Scientific and Cultural Organization). Their subdivisions reach into everyone's daily life without most people even being aware of it. They also have ties to the freemasons, skull and bones, and the knights Templar. **Their ultimate goal is for a one world government that they will control.** Also, a one world currency, and they want to control and ownership of all land, property, resources and people. Also, they **manipulate political parties**, and the legal and illegal drug trade and federal agencies related to all matters listed above." *Rockefeller Foundation, Ford Foundation, Carlisle group, J.P.Morgan, Oppenheimer, Kuhn Leub, federal reserve system and many others involved."* (Bolding and underline added) http://www.urbandictionary.com/define.php?term=Illuminati).

In general, the Illuminati organization is the worldwide communist party leadership controlling communist nations, Islamic nations, United Nations, and the Democratic Party.

PRESIDENT OBAMA: aka Comrade President Obama

Dear reader, this book is in the course of making extraordinary and bold statements about the Democratic Party and their relationship to the World's Communist organizations.

For the record, I am not a conspiratorial person by nature, not one looking for recognition, I am not a knight on a white horse trying to save the world, just an everyday person who loves his country. One who is very concerned as to what is happening to the greatest country on earth, AMERICA. I am worried about the future of families and the future of all the good citizens of this country. Therefore, I have decided to research, learn about the political climate of our times, and bring them out in the open by sharing them with America.

We live in a day of high technology where it is almost impossible to hide the truth from the world. Information on any subject or any person can be found either online or in books written by others who share concerns for truth. That is what I am doing; searching the Internet or reading books by others who have already found information opening up the reality. One book I highly recommend to read is the book titled "Barack Obama and the Enemies Within" by Trevor Loudon, Pacific Freedom Foundation. It is over 600 pages with accurate documentation covering the complete political life of Obama with excellent follow-up documentation. This book will help the reader to understand the truth about who and what Obama believes.

About President Obama; every day we hear someone ask out loud "what is going on with this man." Why is he acting the way he does? Why is he making or refusing to make the kind of decisions that are necessary for the social well-being of his country? Why is he refusing to take the kind of political actions needed to safeguard his country or acting to protect other nations and people especially Christians, and the unborn life of children? The answer is he does not hold the same kind of concerns, passion, or values for this country as most Americans. His religious, political ideology exemplifies Marxism, not the Constitution, and not the "Spirit of America".

Remember on Mar 26, 2012, when President Obama was caught off guard on a hot mic. He told outgoing Russian President Dmitri Medvedev to tell Putin "that if given "space," I'll have more flexibility after my election. Meaning once he wins his second election as President he is in an open and unrelenting position to better cooperate with Putin.

Comrade Obama's commitment is to the principles of communism and the oncoming of a One World Order. His foreign and national policies do not come about by accident. He has an immoral understanding of his country and the world. His foreign and domestic policies provide direct support for Russia, China, Cuba, and Iran in strengthening the movement of global Communism. It is my hope when you finish reading this section on Obama you will have factual evidence and on the understanding that Obama is an entirely dedicated communist.

Comrade Obama is a man filled with controversies in his birth records, college records, family upbringing, college activities, and community involvement. Obama claims he is not a socialist; he is Christian. However, when viewed, not by his words but by his political actions, those claims stand without support. Next, he has the problem of being a pathological liar, a man speaking untruthfully to America on a regular basis.

As for being called a socialist, when the public observes his political acts they speak for themselves. His actions of redistribution, absolute disregard for the Constitution through executive orders and his Obamacare all display works as a religious, political communist. His feelings towards his religion: true religion is action, not one's words, actions tell the real story. When Obama calls Islam a great religion, he is a foolish man, a hypocrite, or one who does not understand what it means to be a Christian. There can only be one true World Religious leader, a proven Jesus Christ or a flawed Muhammad. Over his time in office, Obama has not displayed himself as one being in support of Christianity but one in opposition to Christianity. As the Bible states: Ye shall know them by their fruits (Matthew 7:16).

Speaking about his pathological problems: the list of his lying is ongoing. Both Hitler and Lenin were very familiar with the art of lying. They have said in effect "if you tell a lie often enough the people will start to believe it." Lying is a trait often used by the Democrats, leftist, Islam, the communist style of government. If the truth does not serve their purpose, then it is OK to falsify the truth. Obama has used this tactic often enough that even the press has awarded him at times with the "Pinocchio" award. Have other Presidents lied, yes? However, Obama without question, as of this date, has become the most artful untrustworthy man in the White House to serve America.

While attending the University of Hawaii Stanley Ann Durham (Obama's mother) married Barack Hussian Obama Sr. (Obama's father) and Barack Obama the 2nd was born on August 4, 1961. The marriage of Ann and Obama Sr. lasted only three years. Dunham later met Lolo Soetoro, a Javanese surveyor who had come to Honolulu in September 1962 on an East–West Center grant to study geography at the University of Hawaii. Soetoro graduated from the University of Hawaii with an M.A. in geography in June 1964. In 1965, Soetoro and Dunham were married in Hawaii, and in 1966, Soetoro returned to Indonesia. Dunham graduated from the University of Hawaii with a B.A. in anthropology on August 6, 1967, and moved in October the same year with her six-year-old son to Jakarta, Indonesia, to rejoin her husband.

Ann Dunham and her son Barack lived in Indonesia until 1971. At that time, Ann sent the 10-year-old Obama back to Hawaii so he would be able to attend Punahou Prep School starting in 5th grade rather than having him stay in Indonesia with her.

From that point on Barack Obama lived the remainder of his life without the guidance of a compassionate father.

"In 1995, an aspiring politician named Barack Obama published an autobiography called *Dreams from My Father*. There, Obama acknowledged the people who influenced him throughout his life. Among the most prominent influences was a figure that Obama acknowledged only as "Frank." … As readers of *The Blaze* know, Frank Marshall Davis (1905-87) was a mentor to a young Barack Obama throughout the 1970s, the period of Obama's adolescence. Davis was also a literal card-carrying member of the Communist Party—Party number 47544.

"Davis edited and wrote for Party-line publications such as the *Honolulu Record* and the *Chicago Star*, which included contributors who served as actual agents to Stalin's Soviet Union. Davis did outrageous Soviet propaganda work in his columns, at every juncture agitating and opposing U.S. attempts to slow Joseph Stalin."

(http://www.theblaze.com/contributions/obama%E2%80%99s-purge-why-has-frank-marshall-davis-been-quietly-removed-from-dreams-from-my-father/).

"Davis's political antics were so radical that the FBI placed him on the federal government's Security Index. Which meant he could immediately be detained in the event of a national emergency, such as a war breaking out between the United States and USSR.

"It's hard to imagine that anyone could see Davis as a mentor. And yet, in the autumn of 1970, Davis was introduced to Obama by Obama's grandfather, who was seeking a role model/father figure to mentor his grandson. Davis and Obama would meet throughout the 1970s; right up until Obama left Hawaii for Occidental College in 1979. In fact, in *Dreams from My Father*, Obama notes the parting advice he got from Davis before departing for Occidental; it was a classic Davis diatribe trashing "the American way." (Ibid above)

"Frank" is mentioned throughout Obama's book. Curiously, in the abridged audio version of *Dreams from My Father* released in 2005, the year Obama began his Senate career; all mentions of his mentor were scrubbed. But now this video does exists online. In it, Obama talks about sitting with Davis in his home drinking whiskey listening to him talk about how "black people have a reason to hate… so you might as well get used to it."

Another quote of Davis that Obama included in the book was, "They'll train you so good, you'll start believing what they tell you about equal opportunity and the American way and all that sh*t."

"The 1995 video shows a young Obama expressing his views on what Davis taught him:

"*White Americans… partake in a hybrid culture. The truth of the matter is, that American culture at this point -- that is truly American -- is black culture to a large degree. Flip on the television set, look at "Pulp Fiction" -- you can choose whatever examples you want. It's had a profound influence on this entire nation, and it has to be affirmed… Obama said. "At least theoretically, most conservatives still say that they believe in anti-discrimination laws; they just don't believe in Affirmative Action."*

(http://www.truthrevolt.org/news/1995-video-obama-praises-communist-mentor-frank-marshall-davis).

"LET'S CUT TO THE CHASE: Frank Marshall Davis was a literal, card-carrying member of Communist Party USA (CPUSA). His card number was 47544. He was pro-Soviet, pro–Red China. He edited and wrote for Party-line publications such as the *Chicago Star* and the *Honolulu Record*; contributors to the former served as secret agents to Stalin's Soviet Union. Davis did outrageous Soviet propaganda work in his columns, at every juncture agitating and opposing U.S. attempts to slow Joseph Stalin and Mao Tse-tung. He favored Yalta and Red Army takeovers of Poland, Czechoslovakia, Yugoslavia, and Central and Eastern Europe. He urged America to dump the "fascist," Chiang Kai-shek in support of Mao's Red force. He wanted Communist takeovers in Korea and Vietnam." (http://spectator.org/articles/34799/dreams-frank-marshall-davis).

As early as the 1970's Barack (5th-grade schoolboy), was well on his way to tutoring in the art of religious, political ideology of communism by his mentor Mr. Davis. What is the meaning of the word "mentor" as it relates to Davis and Obama? The dictionary defines the word mentor as "teacher, coach, or as a wise, loyal advisor."

As a wise, devoted teacher and coach what are the things Davis instilled in Obama while preparing his life as a politician? Davis' political religion instructed Obama to:

1. Disbelieve in the founding principles of America, the "Spirit of America."
2. Davis implanted his beliefs in the philosophies of Marxist leadership.
3. Socialism over Capitalism.
4. Public control of industry and property.
5. Religion is subservient (to be used by) to Communism.
6. Disdain for America.

Obama attended Occidental College, Los Angles, and California from 1979 to 1981.

"Americans for Freedom of Information has released copies of President Obamas college transcripts from Occidental College. Released today, the transcript indicates that Obama, under the name Barry Soetoro, received financial aid as an international student from Indonesia as an undergraduate at the school. The transcript was released by Occidental College in compliance with a court order in a suit brought by the group in the Superior Court of California. The transcript shows that Obama (Soetoro) applied for financial aid and was awarded a fellowship for foreign students from the Fulbright Foundation Scholarship program. To qualify, for the scholarship, a student must claim foreign citizenship." Soetoro was his step-father's last name. Barack did not apply for college officially as a citizens of America." (Read at http://www.snopes.com/politics/obama/birthers/occidental.asp#LZeBXE0hB2cTUCV9.99).

As stated by the Constitution, if a person claims to be the citizen of a foreign country that disqualifies one to be the President of the United States. According to Obama's Occidental application, Barack Obama did apply for financial aid as a foreigner and not a citizen of the United States.

During 1981, Barack Obama was a transfer student from California's Occidental College to Columbia University as a 20-year-old college junior and graduated from Columbia in 1983.

The following article by Wayne Allyn Root, (a former classmate of Obama), provides additional insights of Obama's communist indoctrination:

"America's decline under Obama isn't due to mistake, ignorance, or incompetence at the hands of a community organizer. It's a **purposeful**, brilliant plan hatched at Columbia University **to destroy capitalism**, American exceptionalism, Judeo-**Christian values**, and the American Dream. (Bold added).

"What matters is what Obama learned and experienced at Columbia. My classmates hated America. They spoke with glee about one day "taking the system down." They blamed America for "unfairness, racism, inequality, and lack of social justice."

Recognize those words?

"My classmates proudly called themselves socialists, communists, and Marxists. Even though almost all of them came from wealthy families (or perhaps because of it), they hated the rich and despised business owners. They talked about how the "white power structure" had to be dismantled, business owners bankrupted, and capitalism destroyed. Everything in their minds was based on "social justice."

"Does that sound like the policies of anyone you recognize in the White House? Does "We have to spread the wealth around" ring a bell? How about "If you own a business, you didn't build that."

"How about Obama's hatred of Republicans and refusal to negotiate with Congress? It's clear he thinks he's "morally superior" to conservatives. That attitude was born at Columbia too.

"In 1981 when a student burst through the doors to our political science class and screamed. "The President has been shot. They've assassinated Reagan"... my classmates yelled, hugged, high-fived, and jumped up and down cheering the death of a Republican. Today most of my classmates are either in government with Obama or controlling the mainstream media. They talk about "moderation and compromise," but always remember 30 years ago they cheered for the death of a Republican.

"However, there's more. We were all taught a simple, but brilliant plan. My classmates discussed it 24/7. It was their "American Dream."

"It was called "Cloward-Piven," after former Columbia professors Richard Cloward and Frances Piven. **To bring down America and our capitalist system, they were taught to overwhelm the system with massive spending, entitlements and debt. That would cause the economy to collapse, wipe out the middle class, and bring Americans to their knees, begging the government to save them**.

"It's the exact plan Obama has been implementing. The **centerpiece is Obamacare**. Obamacare isn't about healthcare. It's about **bankrupting the middle class** and addicting it to government dependency. It's about redistributing wealth from the middle class and small business to **Obama's voters (the poor and unions)**. Its goal is to **wipe out the last**

vestiges of middle-class America, creating a two-class society: the super-rich and the poor (both beholden to Obama). (Bolding added).

"Obama learned well; it's working to perfection. So that explains the plan. But how do you implement it? We were taught that at Columbia too.

"An essential component of the plan involved <u>fooling the voters</u> by calling yourself "moderate" and a "uniter," even though you are <u>a radical Marxist</u>. We were never taught to admit what you believe in. It involved demonizing your opponents, calling them "evil, greedy, extreme, radical, and terrorist." Look in the mirror and call your opponents the very things you are. Obama learned well." (http://www.theblaze.com/contributions/what-obama-and-i-learned-at-columbia-how-to-destroy-america-from-within/).

NOTE: The "Cloward-Piven," "American Dream", plan consists of the following:

1. Bring down America.
2. Break the Capitalist system.
3. Create <u>massive spending</u>.
4. Create <u>entitlement</u> programs.
5. Create <u>debt</u>.
6. Collapse the economy.
7. Destroy the middle class.
8. Bring America to its knees.

In the below article are selected statements from an interview, "Dr. Drew will, of course, refer to Dr. John Drew and LP will refer to the author of this piece, Louis Puissegur.

(Read more at http://freedomoutpost.com/2012/09/interview-obama-had-marxist-vision-for-us-at-occidental-college/#LwOFI Qe7SWmMleHw.99)

Dr. Drew; "Right, I mean, the way I look at it, Barack Obama was probably at least a Communist sympathizer when he came out of high school, he was **definitely a Marxist revolutionary** when I met him in 1980. It doesn't look like he changed a bit; he started hanging out with Bill Ayers. (Obama a student at Occidental College year of 1981)... Drew; "It is kind of complex, the actual time I spent with Obama was sort of brief and limited, but he was part of my social sphere in the sense I knew his roommate at the time, Chandoo, and Obama was a member of the Democratic Socialist Alliance at Occidental and my girlfriend, Caroline Boss, was the co-president of that organization."

LP; "Democratic Socialist Alliance?"

Dr. Drew; "Yes, that was the **Marxist student association** on campus, Caroline hung up a huge banner of Karl Marx where the students met at the Occidental College Quad. She and I were pretty intense Marxists. We had been involved in about a two-year relationship and she was the one who introduced me to Barack Obama, she knew him better than I did. I wouldn't be saying he was a Marxist/Socialist revolutionary if it was just based with my face to face talk with him, my comments are based on knowing Chandoo, having known Caroline and the **Marxist Professors** and that whole culture."

LP; "Another words, the people he was associated with were deep into the Marxist/Socialist ideology?"

Dr. Drew; "Oh yes, I had considered myself as the enemy of the American government at that time."

LP: "At that particular time? And what made you change?"

Dr. Drew; "Well, the first thing that happened was kind of spiritual change. I just started having the religious experience; I realized that there was something out there which I now call a higher power. That was very inconsistent with Marxist ideology. Because Marxism taught that stuff like that was just the opinion of the people, but to me it was very real, so very real. Then my Doctoral research ended up just confirming a lot of Marxist theory which comes to explain how welfare programs and how Capitalism deals with child labor and things like that. My research pulled me out of Marxism fundamentally but what started it was the spiritual change."

" We hung out with Obama and Chandoo for that day and went out to lunch then we ended up arguing pretty late in the evening about Marxism and politics. Whether or not there would be a revolution, a **Communist-style revolution in the United States**. The key takeaway there is that I may have been one of the first people in the world to confront Barack Obama's kind of silly belief, Marxist idea that there was going to be an inevitable **Communist revolution coming to the United States.**

LP; "Obama was a student there the whole time?"

Dr. Drew; "Yes he was a student at Occidental College, and he was taking classes from Roger Boesche, who was a political theorist on campus. Roger was definitely a Socialist. Most of the students followed him as a Marxist revolutionary, but he was kind of precise with that and did not see himself as a Marxist. "I would say that 100% of the students considered him to be a **Marxist/Socialist**."

While attending Columbia University "In *Dreams from My Father*", Obama writes of the "socialist conferences I sometimes attended at the Cooper Union", and he later recounts attending a Stokely Carmichael speech:

"In search of some inspiration, I went to hear Kwame Toure, formerly Stokely Carmichael of SNCC and Black Power fame, speak at Columbia. At the entrance to the auditorium, two women, one black, one Asian, were selling Marxist literature and arguing with each other about Trotsky's place in history. Inside, Toure was proposing a program to establish ties between Africa and Harlem that would circumvent white capitalist imperialism."

"Cooper Union" is the Cooper Union for the Advancement of Science and Art, a privately funded college in Downtown Manhattan. For many years, from the early 1980s until 2004, Cooper Union was the usual venue of the annual Socialist Scholars Conference-almost certainly what Obama was referring to.

"Socialist Scholars Conference"-now known as Left Forum was for many years the largest socialist gathering in the USA, attracting up to 2,000 participants.

"Socialist Scholars Conference founded by a group of radicals from the City University of New York. Led by sociology professor Bogdan Denitch and chairing the Socialist Scholars Conferences since 1980,

Denitch is an Honorary Chair of the Democratic Socialists of America and has served as DSA's representative to the Socialist International.

"Since DSA's formation in 1982, its City University branch has sponsored and organized the Socialist Scholars Conference. (Democratic Socialists of America is essentially a Marxist organization). The bulk of SSC's organizing committees were having been DSA members, as were many conference speakers.

"Other speakers came from the Communist Party USA and its offshoot. The Committees of Correspondence, the International Socialists, and Freedom Road Socialist Organization as well as independent Marxists, Maoists, Trotskyites, black radicals, gay activists and radical feminists. (Underlining added).

"Barack Obama wrote of "conferences" plural, indicating his attendance was not the result of an accident or youthful curiosity." (http://keywiki.org/index.php/Barack_Obama_and_Democratic_Socialists_of_America).

Tim Jones of the Chicago Tribune, wrote on March 27, 2007, that "Obama's mother was recognized as a "Communist Sympathizer." "She was my touchstone when it comes to how I go about the world of Politics," said Barack Obama. (Read more at http://freedomoutpost.com/2012/09/obama-his-marxist-communist-past-exposed/#V4Jt6EdF67rhaF3F.99).

Obama first received his communist indoctrination by his mother, Ann Durham, as a communist sympathizer, next by Mr. Davis at ages 10 to 18. Part 2 of his programming was carried on as a student at Occidental and Columbia. Here we have an example of how colleges are under the guidance of a Secular Communist Educational Systems. Taxpayer money is raising and educating Communists instead of patriots.

OBAMA linked to Democratic SOCIALISTS of America.

Obama's part 3 in communist development as follows: Writing in the radical (and Democratic Socialists of America-connected) Chicago magazine In These Times, in March 2008, Joel Bleifuss asserted;

"In particular, Obama can be linked to the Democratic Socialists of America (DSA), the Democratic Party-oriented organization that is a member of the Socialist International."

"Democratic Socialists of America (DSA) is the largest socialist organization in the US. It is one of two official U.S. affiliates of the Socialist International. It was formed in 1982 from a merger of the Michael Harrington led Democratic Socialist Organizing Committee and the smaller New American Movement."

"DSA works inside the Democratic Party and has cross-membership with the Communist Party USA, Committees of Correspondence for Democracy and Socialism, Socialist Party USA, and the Green Party USA. (Underling and bold added). DSA has close ties to the radical Institute for Policy Studies, ACORN, Jobs with Justice, Congressional Progressive Caucus and publications including Dissent, The Nation, and The American Prospect". (Bold and underline added). (http://keywiki.org/index.php/Barack_Obama_and_Democratic_Socialists_of_America).

NOTE: Once again we find statements tying communist organizations infiltrating the Democratic Party.

Obama Was Hand Picked by Alice Palmer to Succeed Her in the Illinois State Senate.

"In 1995, Alice Palmer represented the state's 13th District and decided to run for the United States Congress. Alice hand-picked Barack Obama to run to replace her for her Senate seat in Illinois.

"Palmer introduced her chosen successor to a few of the district's influential liberals at the home of two well-known figures on the local left: William Ayers and Bernardine Dohrn, former members of the **terrorist Weather Underground**.

"I remember being one of a small group of people who came to Bill Ayers' house to learn that Alice Palmer was stepping down from the Senate and running for Congress," says Quentin Young, a prominent Chicago physician, and advocate for single-payer health care. "(Palmer) identified (Obama) as her successor."

"Ten years earlier, Palmer was an executive board member of the U.S. Peace Council, which the FBI identified as **a communist front group**, an affiliate of the World Peace Council, a Soviet front group. (Bolding added).

"Palmer participated in the World Peace Council's 1983 Prague Assembly, part of the Soviet launch of the nuclear-freeze movement. The only thing it would have frozen was the Soviet Union's military superiority.

"In June 1986, while editor of the Black Press Review, she wrote an article for the Communist Party USA's newspaper, the People's Daily World, now the People's Weekly World. It detailed her experience attending the 27th Congress of the Communist Party of the Soviet Union and how impressed she was by the Soviet system." (http://theobamafile.com/_associates/AlicePalmer.htm).

"She was the only African-American journalist to travel to the **Soviet Union** to attend the 27th Congress of the **Communist Party** of the **Soviet Union**, according to an article Palmer wrote in the **CPUSA** newspaper, People's Daily World, June 19, 1986." Source: Jim Corsi, WorldNetDaily based on Communism in Chicago and the Obama Connection (Cliff Kincaid and Herbert Romerstein). (Bold added).

"Obama's run for the Illinois State Senate was launched by a fund-raiser organized at Ayers' and Dorhn's Chicago home by Alice Palmer. Palmer had named Obama to succeed her in the state Senate in 1995 when she decided to run for a U.S. congressional seat." Source: Jim Corsi, WorldNetDaily based n Communism in Chicago and the Obama Connection." (Cliff Kincaid and Herbert Romerstein).

When Obama ran for the Illinois State Senate, remember he was selected by the Marxist Alice Palmer and then funded by communist organizations.

RUSSIAN INTELLIGENCE

"After Viktor Suvorov, a former Russian intelligence analyst defected to England, he revealed Russia's top-secret plans to attack the United States at some future date after **undermining the United States from within through the subversion of their political leadership.** Suvorov had worked as a Russian intelligence analyst as well as having worked for the GRU and with elite Russian special forces. Suvorov, warned the Americans of <u>Russia's true intentions</u> after the Russian high command had succeeded in getting Pentagon officials to let down their guard and engage in a high level, but mostly one-sided, technology transfer. Under the **wrong President (i.e. Obama)**, <u>America would be weakened</u> to the point to where it could not adequately defend herself... <u>From within, American leadership</u> would be compromised in key positions, and the fall of America would be orchestrated from within and under the leadership of an **Obama** type of President." (Bold and underlining added).

(http://www.dcclothesline.com/2014/04/01/obama-manifestation-multi-generational-soviet-plot-destroy-america/).

We are learning from a former Russian intelligence analyst, America will fall after undermining the United States through subversion of our political leadership by someone like Obama, who is a member of the Democratic Party, selected by the Communist Party USA, with help by Sam Webb Chairman, and Communist support for Obama reelection bid. (Bold and underline added) (Source: http://citizenwells.com/2011/08/04/obama-endorsed-by-communist-party-usa-sam-webb-chairman-communist-support-for-obama-reelection-bid/).

On April 27, 2009, Pravda, The Moscow Communist daily newspaper declared "the American decent into Marxism is happening with **breathtaking speed...The final collapse has come with the election of Barack Obama."** (Bold added).

Ezra Taft Benson's book *"An Enemy Hath Done This"*, foreword page, states, **"if our nation is destroyed, it will be because of internal forces** of fiscal irresponsibility, subversion, and lawlessness, rather than by conquest or assault from any enemy without." (Bold added).

On April 9, 2009, The Cato Institute posted the following:

"While it's a crucial fact, the full story on the Common Core isn't that the feds coerced adoption. It is that the end game is almost certainly **complete federal control** by connecting national standards and tests to annual federal funding. And that, it is now quite clear, is no conspiracy theory." www.cato.org <u>(Bold added)</u>

"Did The Communist Party USA Take Over The Democratic Party in 1988?

"Let's objectively look into this question. **What evidence is there that the CPUSA, Communist Party USA, took over the Democratic Party in 1988?**If the Communist Party had effectively infiltrated and gained control of the Democratic Party, then one would expect them to stop running their own candidates for President and endorse/co-nominate the Democrat nominees for President. There is no way that happened, right? Let's look just in case." (Bold added) (List at http://aun-tv.com/2015/08/did-the-communist-party-usa-take-over-democratic-party-in-1988/).

"Shockingly since 1988 the CPUSA has stopped running their own candidates and have 100% of the time nominated the Democrat candidates as their candidates. So we have to take this question seriously. Have the Communists/Marxists/Socialists ever admitted that Democrats are a front group for them, that the Democrats have adopted their policies, so there is no need to run their own candidates? Multiple Marxist Parties have.

"Norman Thomas, the six-time Socialist Party candidate for U.S. President, said the following in a 1944 speech: "I no longer need to run as a Presidential Candidate for the Socialist Party. **The Democratic Party has adopted our platform."** How about now, not 1944? What does the current Communist Party USA have to say?

"*Sam Webb, the leader of the* **Communist Party USA** *(CPUSA), came out to* **support** *President Barack Obama's re-election in 2012. Webb said that with Obama's victory "that is the ground on which people fight going forward."* With "the emergence of a multi-racial, male-female, working-class based electoral coalition that has the potential to transform America in the years and decades ahead."

"Have any foreign Communists admitted the Democratic Party is a tool of their objectives? Russian propaganda machine RIA Novosti stated that Dimitry Peskov, press secretary for Russian President Vladimir Putin, said: "For Russia, Obama's victory will be beneficial."

And:

"Lieutenant General Ion Mihai Pacepa, a defected former top aide to the Romanian Communist regime, said that an **alliance between the Democratic Party and the Communist Party is underway in America.** Pacepa explained: "The Democratic Party has become dangerously <u>infected</u> with the <u>Marxism virus</u>. I recognize the symptoms because I once lived through them—-

"So **Marxists say the Democratic Party is a Marxist party**, what do Democrats say? **Bernie Sanders is an admitted Marxist.** Since a publicly admitted Marxist (Bernie Sanders) is now #1 for President in latest polls for Iowa and New Hampshire Democrats, that answers that question as to what Democrats have to say about it." (Polls as of October 6, 2015). (Bold added)

(http://beforeitsnews.com/politics/2015/08/did-the-communist-party-usa-take-over-democratic-party-in-1988-2735104.html).

CPUSA touts are to support the Democratic Party issues. Entire story at http://aun-tv.com/2015/08/did-the-communist-party-usa-take-over-democratic-party-in-1988/.

The announcement came from Party Chairman Sam Webb during a web streaming event called "Taking care of the future: from here to socialism." (See more at: http://www.teaparty.org/communist-party-usa-tells-obama-were-got-back-34813/#sthash.ORf9nnMJ.dpuf).

Party chief says, "Thanks to Obama America is more willing to embrace communist ideals." According to Webb, Communists are planning something similar whereby they would unite with left-wing groups to protect President Obama and his Democrats from losing the Senate to the tea party. I don't see how it's going to happen without a much stronger left, and an important part of that left is a bigger stronger Communist Party. That's a necessary component. He also noted that the "**Communist Party USA was an integral part of FDR'S New Deal policies.**"

"According to the Center for Military Readiness, the U.S. military is in jeopardy because it is being subjected to a radical social experimentation being forced upon it. The U.S. military has seen generals and other high-level officers relieved of duty at an unprecedented rate during the

Obama administration…**Obama has inflicted** "great damage" to our U.S. military. He has taken away critical resources and imposed "heavy burdens of social experimentation" upon them."(Bolding added)

(http://www.teaparty.org/communist-party-usa-tells-obama-weve-got-back-34813/).

OBAMA'S IMMIGRATION POLICES

"We have immigration laws in this country for two basic reasons: to pre-serve American jobs and to protect national security. President Barack Obama's unlawful executive actions to grant amnesty to at least 5 million illegal immigrants violate both of those principles. Any objective review must find that the president's policies have placed the concerns of those who have broken our laws **ahead of the interests of citizens** and legal residents of the United States." (Bold added) (http://www.rollcall.com/news/obama_policies_favor_illegal_immigrants_over_american_citizens_commentary-240865-1.html).

"The Results Are In: Obama Never Intended to Enforce Immigration Laws. Using preliminary numbers, the Associated Press reports that de-portations are down to the lowest level in nearly a decade… initially pla-teaued under Obama, and are now collapsing."

"The White House has essentially prohibited immigration agents from doing their jobs, which is a big part of why DHS employee morale is so low.

"It's now indisputable that this administration had no intention of enforcing immigration law tomorrow if it was given an amnesty today. Obama's promises of future enforcement, never very credible, are now exposed as lies.

(Read more at: http://www.nationalreview.com/corner/425165/results-are-in-obama-never-intended-to-enforce-immigration-laws).

Comrade Obama's, the Middle East, communist foreign policies have failed to such an extent that over 12 million refugees are fleeing Syria to find safety, creating a security crisis for Europe, while Obama wants to bring 100,000 Syrian refugees to America. However, because of the 11/13/15 Paris massacre, killing at least 128 in gunfire and blasts, America is calling for the postponement of all refugees to be allowed into our country.

Comrade Obama is telling America to refuse refugees is not within the character of America's values and principles. However, since when did he start to worry about America's values? What about his values when using the IRS to prevent conservative organizations awarded tax status, or when lying about Obama care, or when lying about Benghazi, and especially when attacking Christian values. His entire purpose in office has been to destroy the values of America and the American family.

The problem is that anywhere from 2-5% of the 100,000 refugees will create 2,000 to 5,000 terrorists in Amerca putting America in danger. Again this will work to the advantage of the Democratic Party in breaking down the values and safety of America; something Obama has no feelings or concerns for his country. The FBI also states that over 85% of the Muslims are teaching hate of America inside their Mosque right here in our neighborhoods. Again why would Comrade Obama be willing to allow Islam Mosque teaching hate of America? Another proven statement how Obama offers no sincere feelings for America and the citizens of his country.

Why would Comrade Obama want to bring terrorists to his home country? The answer, to advance communism when bringing people who are raised by indoctrination under Islamic Communism to this country and to add pressure to the Constitution. Within time, Muslims will add stress to our legal system allowing them to be ruled by Sharia Law in place of the Constitution. Thereby, continuing to cause the Constitution to fall apart little by little, one step at a time.

"FBI Director James Comey delivered a stunning estimate of 900 investigations currently in progress against suspected ISIS operatives, recruits, and individuals "inspired" by the Islamic State, and the number of investigations is slowly growing." (http://www.breitbart.com/national-security/2015/10/23/fbi-directo). Please note this is taking place in 50 states in America, not the Middle East.

America, is there need for more information to prove Obama does not have a sincere concern and love for his country?

What is Obama's purpose or reason for not enforcing our immigration laws?

Obama's immigration laws are designed to:

1. Destroy the voting middle class.
2. Bring to America future communist voters.
3. Gain political domination over America.
4. Destroy the financial strength of the country.
5. Keep Blacks and Hispanics in poverty.
6. Increase the number of people who depend on entitlements.
7. Weaken the American family.
8. Breakdown America as a super power.
9. Breakdown America's Constitution.
10. Destroy the "Spirit of America".

After reading the various quotes and facts, presented in this book, might there be reasons for sincere concerns about Clinton, Obama, and the Democratic Party supporting Communism and not representing America, the Constitution, or the citizens of this country? Facts show they do serve the Communist Party in their design to gain power and control of the United States of America.

In our upcoming election, the question to ask is where do the voters stand? Will citizens vote for America or Communism? Vote for the Communist Democratic Party or vote for the parties and candidates committed to the Constitution? Vote for a communist government or vote for Liberty and free agency? Is America voting as a Frog or for Liberty?

WRAPPING-UP:

1. Communism is government power and control over people.
2. Managing the agency of man is the bottom line.

3. Agency is the right to make independent choices without compulsion.
4. Controlling a person's behavior is a communist goal.
5. Communism must control government laws and religion.
6. Communism is working to destroy the "Spirit of America": God, Family, and Constitution.
7. America is becoming the Boiling Frog Syndrome.
8. Democrats removed God from their 2014 Political platform.
9. Mayflower: communism is leading to slavery.
10. America's Communist Party has created spy organizations since 1919.
11. Soviet Union infiltrated the White House in 1930 with FDR's open arms policies.
12. FDR freely turned over our nuclear programs to Russia.
13. FDR's New Deal socialists programs extended the Great Depression by over seven years.
14. FDR advanced Russia as a world Superpower.
15. Dr. Cleon Skousen alerted America of the Communist Goals to destroy America.
16. USA Communist Party has captured the Democratic Party.
17. The Kremlin's KBG trained President Clinton.
18. Clinton's Secret Service agents were members of the Communist Party.
19. Clinton disarmed our military by 50%.
20. Clinton assisted China in obtaining nuclear secrets.
21. Clinton was a secret Illuminist.
22. Clinton says America will get used to communism.
23. Bill, Hillary, and Democratic Party linked to Marxism.
24. Illuminati organization is the ultimate goal of a One World order.
25. Obama's communist indoctrination started with his mother Ann; Davis then schooled at Occidental and Columbia.
26. It is a proven fact Obama was a member of communist organizations.

27. Communist organizations supported Obama's elections.
28. Marxism says the Democrat Party is a Marxist party.
29. Russian intelligence confirms communist organizations are undermining America.
30. Pravda, Moscow's major newspaper, states that Obama's election is the final steps in the collapse of America.
31. Marxism confirms the Democratic Party is a Marxist Party.
32. Obama's purpose for illegal immigration is to destroy America and the middle-class, keep minorities in poverty, and weaken the American family.
33. Obama plans to overrun this country with Muslims with their communist non-American values.

CHAPTER 3

—— § ——

Democratic/Communism Tools For Implementing Communism

The Only Thing Necessary for the Triumph of Evil is that Good Men Do Nothing.

EDMUND BURKE

STATED EARLIER THERE are only two Political Religious ideologies that exist in the world. One ideology based on God's government, the second is the Political Religion based on Man's way of thinking. God's religion yielding freedom versus Man's religion controls liberty. Also, evidence was presented showing the Democratic Party is moving America in the footsteps of World Communism.

Beginning with Lenin and Stalin right up to today's events, the World Communist organization has been infiltrating America's political institutions seeking to gain control of the United States.

It started with President Roosevelt allowing his White House to be overrun with Russian Spies, providing for and turning over full nuclear capabilities to Moscow, and relinquishing massive amounts of military-political control of immeasurable amounts of territory to Stalin.

President Bill Clinton, an associate member of the Illuminati's group, received preparation from the KGB before becoming our 42nd President. His personal security team consisted of Marxist followers, and he allowed the turning over of valuable military and nuclear support to China.

Bill Clinton is possibly one of the least decent men to be the President of the United States. Clinton has been accused of multiple sexual assaults starting as a Rhodes Scholar at Oxford in 1969 right up to White House. Because of his sexual problems Congress impeached Clinton, charging him with lying under oath to a federal grand jury and obstructing justice. (http://www.freerepublic.com/focus/news/1157708/posts).

Today we are witnessing President Obama transforming America into a Communist Constitutional scheme. Actions displayed by Obama support his aversion and disgust for our Constitution and the "Christian Spirit of America." His particular activities, domestic and foreign policies, are for the purpose of supporting a One World Communist Order. Several examples include opening relations with Communist Cuba, militarily pulling back on the conflict in the Middle East, and allowing Russia to gain control while refusing to avert China from gaining Naval strength of the Asia-Pacific trade route territory.

Obama's economic policies are purposely destroying the middle-class designed to bring America to the brink of a financial collapse (a key goal of the Communist mission). In 1971, 61% of families were classified as middle-income households. Today Pew Research Center states that is currently at 50%. His creation of a communist health program is intended to control America's health agenda. Next by opening the door for Iran to receive 150 billion dollars Iran will become the major threat to the Middle East stability. Each policy is designed to fulfill Obama's premeditated purpose of supporting Communism's world dominance.

Today's Democratic Party Leaders are using an arsenal of tools to gain control over the American people, and the Constitution. Let's start by referring to the article listing the 45 "Communist Goals (1963) Congressional Record--Appendix, pp. A34-A35 January 10, 1963" read in Congress for the purpose of alerting the public to the dangers of communism in America.

NOTE: The three most dictatorial goals of the Communist Party are to destroy the Religion of Jesus Christ, the **Family**, and the Constitution.

When reviewing the 45 Communist goals, unquestionably, they are intended to accomplish each of those primary objectives. The following numbered points are specially designed to fulfill their mission in America:

#16 Control courts	#17 Control schools
#21 Entertainment	#24 Promote Obscenity
#25 Pornography	#26 Homosexuality
#27 Infiltrate Churches	#28 Eliminate Prayer
#29 Constitution	#30 Discredit Founders
#32 Entitlements	#40 Discredit Family
	#41 Discredit Parents

#4. "**Permit free trade between all nations regardless of Communist affiliation and regardless of whether or not items could be for war.**" Goal: to move manufacturing jobs from America to Communist countries, creating a loss of job and income security, and to create family instability.

For example, NAFTA led to the loss of some 625,000 jobs in the U.S., thanks to companies moving across the border to Mexico. (when.com/Disadvantages+Nafta+Mexico).

America's national defense resources are being made available to communist countries at a cost of developing Russia, China, and Iran into world military powers. *Win Communism*.

6. "**Provide American aid to all nations regardless of Communist domination**." During the year 2012, the American taxpayer shelled out $37,680,000,000 in foreign aid. WHY? Our current national deficient is now $19 trillion. Last year U.S.A. spent $430 billion on interest payments alone. Every year, taxpayers are paying $3,500 per person on interest. This money could be used to pay for roads, bridges, education, medical research, defense, and to help the poverty-stricken and undernourished children.

Each American has a national debt responsibility of $56,604,000. We are financially strengthening communist countries that dislike and cry out DEATH TO AMERICA.

Win Communism.

#11. "**Promote the U.N. and demand as a one-world government.**" Allowing Communist leaders (through world courts, committee groups, and treaties) to take control of America. The U.N. is the headquarters for a "One World Government", for the ILLUMINATI.
 Win Communism.

#15. "*Capture one or both of the political parties in the United States.*" This goal has been successfully achieved with the elections of Clinton and Obama. *Win Communism.*

#16. "**Use courts to weaken basic American institutions.**" The goal has been accomplished as of 1960 through courts dealing with schools, religion, individual agency**,** and **moral** issues.
 Win Communism.

#17. "**Getting control of schools**." Achieving this goal allows the use of schools to be used as a transmission for Communist/Iran propaganda.
 Softening the curriculum and getting control of teachers associations are two additional strategies used to get control of schools. Teacher organizations and Common Core Education programs are increasing control of our schools. According to Business Insider Education report for Ranking of Top Countries in Reading, Science, Math, 2013, America ranks 35th in math, 23rd in reading, and 27th in science. Each American ranking is **far below** the world average. American students are some of the lowest performing educated students worldwide.
 (http://www.businessinsider.com/pisa-rankings-2013-12).

"Antonio Gramsci, a communist leader, analyzed Western culture and concluded that the only way that communists could finally impose their totalitarian will over the West was first **taking over its educational**, cultural and **religious** institutions. This would require years of stealthful infiltration". (Bold added) (Read more at http://www.wnd.com/2000/09/103/ #PwCjApw2kbviPXeb.99). *Win Communism*.

#20**. "Infiltrate the press."** Currently, 80-90% of our news agencies consist of Liberal reporters or correctly stated Democratic Party supporters, in short supporters of the communist agenda. It is so unfortunate that today's press is willing to give away their constitutional freedom while destroying their Country's liberties. They must understand if this country comes to be controlled by Communism; the Press will lose their Constitutional freedom of the Press as in Russia and China.

Win Communism.

#21. "**Gain control of key positions in radio, TV, and motion pictures."** Moral standards in TV and motion pictures have reached an all-time ethical low, designed to destroy the family.

Win Communism.

#22. "**Continue discrediting American culture."** Some examples of this strategy are by degrading all forms of Christian art expression, removing all Christian Religious **crosses** and statues from public areas, and "eliminating all moral sculptures from parks and buildings, and substituting with shapeless, awkward and meaningless forms." Accomplished/ Ongoing since 1960. *Win Communism*.

#24**. "Eliminate all laws governing obscenity** by calling them "censorship" and a violation of free speech and free press." This goal is accomplished with the help of the ACLU, American United, and anti-Constitutional judges. *Win Communism*.

#25. "**Break down cultural standards of morality by promoting pornography** and obscenity in books, magazines, motion pictures, radio, and TV: Calling them "censorship," a violation of free speech, and free press." This ongoing breakdown of cultural standards is designed to destroy religion and family values currently ongoing. _Win Communism_.

#27. **"Infiltrate the churches and replace revealed religion with "social" religion. Discredit the Bible** and emphasize the need for intellectual maturity, which does not need a "religious crutch." To accomplish this goal, Communists, have infiltrated the World Christian Council (WCC). _Win Communist_.

(The following article is about the WCC located at http://cnview.com/on_line_resources/world_council_of_churches.htm).

"Do not forget for one minute, however, that when WCC leaders speak and WCC pronouncements are issued IT IS ALWAYS THE VOICE OF RADICALISM AND REVOLUTION THAT IS HEARD. There are repeated attacks upon "Western Imperialism" and "capitalism" but seldom a word of criticism of socialism and communism. Noncommunist dictatorships are repeatedly attacked, but no word is ever spoken against the communist dictators. A few conservative voices are occasionally heard within WCC meetings - but these rarely, if ever, become a part of the official statements that go to the governments of the world and the United Nations as a "representative voice of the churches." Those who claim that the WCC is becoming more "evangelical" are either blind or naive. Evangelicals who remain in the WCC are being used as window dressing to hide the WCC apostasy.

"IN JAMAICA, A PRIME TOPIC OF DISCUSSION WAS THE $85,000 GRANT TO THE PATRIOTIC FRONT OF ZIMBABWE (**actually a communist guerilla group**)... Over three million dollars has been given to radical groups around the world. While it claimed that all monies in this fund come from designated gifts, this program could not operate without the administrative offices and support of the WCC.

"THE WORLD COUNCIL OF CHURCHES AND THE UNITED NATIONS continues their close ties. In fact, we might call them "blood brothers"... The WCC issued a special document promoting the UN-sponsored

International Year of the Child, totally ignoring the fact that even though this appeal is made with the image of starving children in mind, the real thrust of this program is toward socialization of the child and the family." (Bolding added). (http://cnview.com/on_line_resources/world_council_of_churches.htm.). Again *Win Communism*.

Today many Christian churches are directing their attention in creating socialized secular religion, versus faith-based religion, as guided by Communist suggestions.

#28. "**Eliminate prayer or any phase of religious expression in the schools** on the ground that it violates the principle of "separation of church and state." Supreme Court decisions have eliminated forms of prayer on school grounds. Morality, crime rates, and family values have significantly deteriorated with the removal of religious expression in the schools. *Win Communism*.

#29. "**Discredit the American Constitution** by calling it inadequate, old-fashioned, out of step with modern needs, a hindrance to cooperation between nations on a worldwide basis."

Just how do the leaders of the United States and the Supreme Court feel about the Constitution?

"Seven years before Barack Obama's "spread the wealth" comment to Joe the Plumber became a GOP campaign theme, the Democratic presidential candidate said in a radio interview the U.S. has suffered from a **fundamentally flawed Constitution** that does not mandate or allow for redistribution of wealth."

(Bold and underlining added)Read more at (http://www.wnd.com/2008/10/79225/#6c84yB8hDZe7yCT9.99).

"In a television interview during a visit to Egypt last week (12/02/2008), Justice Ruth Bader Ginsburg of the Supreme Court seemed to agree. "I would not look to the United States Constitution if I were drafting a constitution in the year 2012," she said. She recommended, instead, the South African Constitution, the Canadian Charter of Rights and

Freedoms or the European Convention on Human Rights."... **The United States Constitution is terse and old,** and it guarantees relatively few rights." (Bolding and underlining added)(http://hubpages.com/forum/topic/92541).

Our Founding Fathers (George Washington, John Adams, and Benjamin Franklin) numerous times stated the very "hand of God" was upon the creation of the Constitution. However, it appears Obama and Ginsburg's intellect, far exceed the wisdom of God's Constitution.

The question is if our leaders do not believe in the Constitution, what about the citizens of this country? How about Yale students signing a partition to remove the First Amendment from the Constitution? *Win Communist*.

30. **"Discredit the American Founding Fathers**. Present them as selfish aristocrats who had no concern for the "common man."

To say there was no concern for the ordinary man is a gross miscalculation of these men. The entire reason to fight England was for the common man and all future generations. Why is it important for Communism to discredit these men? They do not want citizens believing in American Exceptionalism. To do so means we believe in a Higher Power besides man and the Communist government. If citizens follow our founders and their American principles, Communism will be eliminated.

Win America.

#31. "**Belittle all forms of American culture and discourage the teaching of American history** on the ground that America is only a minor part of the "big picture."

To the contrary, history supports America as the greatest part of the world picture, the dominant element of world history since World War One. Also, during the millennium, Communism will not exist upon the earth.

Those who have viewed Bill O'Rielly's "Waters" interviewing the public, quickly realize America does not remember America and its history.

The majority of today's American citizens do not have a fundamental knowledge of the history of their country. <u>Win Communism.</u>

America is currently and will continue to struggle through tough times until it is willing to overpower the false concepts of Communism. America needs to remembers the quote, "<u>Blessed is the Nation whose God is the Lord.</u>" (Psalms 33:12). If America returns to these exceptional fundamental beliefs, America will become free from those who fail to know and understand the God of this land.

#32. "**Support any socialist movement** to give centralized control (Federal government) over any part of the culture--**education, social agencies, welfare programs,** mental health clinics." The above programs are currently under the control of Obama and his party. Their intent is to bring about a rise in poverty, family failure, racial tensions, moral decay, a breakdown in work ethics, and National financial instability. _Win Communism._

#40. "**Discredit the family as an institution**. Encourage promiscuity and easy divorce."

The discrediting of families began in 1969 when California passed the first unilateral no-fault divorce laws that said one person could leave a marriage without the spouse's consent and a particular violation. Within 15 years, similar laws had been passed nationwide. In 1960, the U.S. Census said 1.8 percent of men and 2.6 percent of women were divorced. By 2011, it had jumped to 9 percent of men and 11 percent of women.

According to Family Edge – a larger number of single moms are living with partners. They report, 58% of all unmarried births now occur to cohabiting couples, compared to 41% in 2002.

(http://www.mercatornet.com/family_edge/view/married_parents_vs_cohabiting_parents/14633#sthash.ArnjMjb0.dpuf.).

Win Communism.

#41. "**Emphasize the need to raise children away from the influence of parents.** According to <u>"Win Communism"</u>, each year schools and local authorities in America are usurping more and more of the rights of the parents. They take the position that once the child is dropped off at the school, the school is in charge, not the parents. Today's many schools counsel students on issues of abortion, drugs, sex, family lifestyle, and marriage, all without the consent of the parents. They instruct students about communist social issues like homosexuality of two dads or two moms.

Everyday schools are making life caring decisions without the consent of the parents. Below are three, out of a long list, such decisions by schools without the acknowledgment of the parents:

First, "some states require notification of the teenager's parents, some require consent from one or both parents and some states have no policy. In the states with no policy, there is no consent or notification needed. A 13-year-old can get an abortion without notification to her parents." (http://parentingteens.about.com/od/teenpregnancy/f/abortionlaws.htm.).

Second, a "mother was furious after she had said her 15-year-old daughter's school arranged an <u>abortion</u> for her daughter without her knowledge." (http://abcnews.go.com/Health/teen-abortion-high-school/story?id=10189694) (Underling added).

Third, the "issue appears to be particularly fraught in the <u>21 states</u> where minors are allowed to have IUDs implanted without parental consent. Most of those states do not distinguish by age in granting youth autonomous birth-control rights, which means kids as young as 11 could be given access." (http://www.theatlantic.com/education/archive/2015/09/student-health-centers-schools-contraception/403954/).
Win Communism.

#26. "Present homosexuality, degeneracy and promiscuity as "normal, natural, and healthy."

This goal is designed to destroy religion and family values. The leading party to support homosexuality is the Democratic Party. <u>Win Communism.</u>

The following article is from *"Homosexual 'Equality': One Step in Destroying Freedom"* **is a must read for all Americans and especially the Democratic Voters.**

"When the Supreme Court on Wednesday issued its ruling gutting the Defense of Marriage Act and allowing a lower-court ruling against California's ban on homosexual marriage to stand, gay activists and their supporters saw it as a victory for "equality"... Another way to look at it is as the culmination of a long-term political strategy to destroy freedom in the United States.

"According to Skousen, communists in the 1950s had 45 long-range goals for bringing about the collapse of the United States' society and leading to its replacement by a communist dictatorship. A perusal of the list reveals activities that are well-known and documented to have taken place over the past half century, such as the infiltration of the media, and schools and unions by communists and socialists. Some of the most disturbing are the goals that describe efforts to manipulate social attitudes.

"But it is undeniable that there is an influential **communist/socialist** movement under the surface of American politics, particularly on the Left. Nancy Pelosi and many other prominent Democrats are members of the <u>Congressional Progressive Caucus</u>, whose web page was hosted by the <u>Democratic Socialists of America, a communist group</u>, until 1999. The page can still be found in Internet archives. President Barack Obama was a **dues-paying member of the Socialist New Party** in the 1990s, a fact that is hotly denied to this day by his supporters. ***It is also undeniable that the Democratic Party has been the prime mover in normalizing homosexual marriage for political gain."***

"Karl Marx, the founder of communism, stated many times that for his communist revolution to come about, it would **require abolishing the traditional family**. His plan for doing that was to promote promiscuity, divorce, and infidelity. He practiced what he preached, virtually abandoning his own family, and communist leaders in many countries have followed his example.

"Marx was well aware of what a shocking idea he was proposing. "<u>Abolition of the family</u>! Even the most radical flare up at this infamous proposal of the Communists," he wrote.

"One of the first things communists have done in every country after they've taken over is to **go after the <u>churches and undermine religious traditions regarding marriage</u>.** The Soviet Union was infamous for its divorce rate, which far exceeded the United States even in its worst years.

"**<u>Divorce, abortion and the encouragement of promiscuity are key plans in the communist playbook</u>** wherever the philosophy of communism or of socialism — which is just communism in a user-friendly wrapper — take hold.

"Historically, communist countries have tended to persecute homosexuals. In the Soviet Union, they were rounded up and put in mental institutions as dangers to society. In democratic countries, however, **<u>promoting</u>** <u>homosexuality</u> has been a central plank for socialist parties for decades." (Bolding and underlining added)

(Read more at http://patriotupdate.com/homosexual-equality-one-step-in-destroying-freedom/).

"Four-in-ten Americans (42%) said that being gay or lesbian is "just the way some choose to live," while a similar share (41%) said that "people are born gay or lesbian," according to the most recent Pew Research Center poll on the issue, conducted in 2013.

"Fewer U.S. adults (8%) said that people are gay or lesbian due to their upbringing while another one-in-ten (9%) said they did not know or declined to give a response.

"In 1977, only 12% believed Gays were born that way. As of 2014, that opinion has increased more than three times with 42% now believing gays are born that way."

(http://www.pewresearch.org/fact-tank/2015/03/06/americans-are-still-divided-on-why-people-are-gay/).

<u>Yes, Win Communism.</u>

Today Americans are very perplexed on the gay issue while being in step with the goals of the Communist Party to destroy the family. However, if America would only take the time and medically study this issue out, they will come to understand two key points: First it is a scientific fact that homosexuality does not connect to DNA or genetics. Second, therefore, individuals are not born gay; homosexuality is politically instituted by the far left and the Communist Party working through the Democratic Party.

Both the far left and the Communist Party have indoctrinated this nation, using the courts and physiological warfare, to brainwash America to be sympathetic towards this issue. It is their desire to destroy the foundation of our society the family. Moreover, it is working!

Historical Overview of the Homosexual Movement

From the mid-1900's and up to 1972, the American Psychiatric Association (APA), classified homosexuality as a "pathological disorder" (emotional disorder). "This action caused the gay community to realize the need to force the APA to take homosexuality off its list of disorders" (*Homosexuality: A Freedom Too Far*, Charles W. Socarides, MD, 1995, page 73).

By 1973, gay activists/communists, working with "Dr. Robert L. Spitzer, successfully had homosexuality "removed" from the APA Psychiatric manual. This clinical diagnosis was replaced with "ego-dystonic homosexuality," meaning that if homosexual attractions were distressful to the individual, they had the right to psychological care." (Socarides, 1995, p. 73).

"The APA could only take the action it did by disregarding and **dismissing hundreds of psychiatric and psychoanalytic research** papers and reports that had been done on homosexuality over the previous two decades…The APA *__ignored the science__* and, for **reasons that were nothing but political**, 'cured' homosexuality by fiat"(done by decree or arbitrary order). (Socarides, 1995, p. 73-74. Bold and underlining added).

Why did the APA give in so easily to political assault, and were willing to **__overturn proven research?__** First, it was just plain easier to give in than to fight the abounding pressure by the homosexual/communist movement. Second, there were members of the APA, who were themselves living this lifestyle. Plain and simple, it was easier for the leadership to switch than fight.

Doctor A. Dean Byrd, Ph.D., MPH, confirms that "by a vote of 5,854 to 3,810 homosexuality was eliminated, as a diagnosis category from the psychiatric manual; making it the **first time** in the history of healthcare, that a diagnosis was decided by popular vote rather than by scientific evidence." (Bold and underlining added)(Setting The Record Straight, Dr. A. Dean Byrd, 2008, page 22).

Even gay activist Simon LeVay "admitted that science did not support the removal" of homosexuality from the diagnostic manual. He noted, "Gay activism was clearly the force that propelled the APA to declassify homosexuality" (*LeVay, S. 1996. Queer Science. Cambridge, Massachusetts: The MIT Press, p. 224*). (Bold added).

In 1974, "the APA supported the removal of the diagnosis from the psychiatric manual with the stipulation that research will be conducted to justify the removal. "No such research has ever been done to justify such a removal" (R. H. & Cummings,

N. A., eds., 2005, Destructive Trends in Mental Health, Cambridge, Massachusetts: Routledge, p. 9).

By 2003, Dr. Robert L. Spitzer produced a study (the same Spitzer who helped to remove homosexuality from the psychoanalytic manual in 1973) published in the *Archives of Sexual Behavior*. Based on his research, "Spitzer concludes that homosexuality is not invariably fixed in all people."

(Hershberger, S. L. 2003. "Guttman Scalability Confirms the Effectiveness of Reparative Therapy." Archives of Sexual Behavior. 32, 5, p. 440). (Bold and underlining added).

The above information presents a brief, but critical, overview of the gay activist, communist political movement. The time has come to no longer align with the clever, rationalized demise offered by the gay and lesbian communist political movement based on the following seven actual, true-to-life reasons:

1. Such "rationalization" is detrimental to the well-being and development of the person who lives this lifestyle.

2.   It undermines the "role of nature."
3.   It enables the erosion of the "nuclear family" and of society.
4.   Genetically it is self-eliminating.
5.   It violates the standards of the Lord.
6.   Homosexuality is a "pathological disorder".
7.   Reorientation therapy offers a 90% possibility for individuals to adjust to a heterosexual lifestyle.

About biological theories, "J. I. Downey states, "At clinical conferences one often hears…that homosexual orientation is fixed and modifiable. Neither assertion is true. The claim that homosexuality is genetic is so reductionist that it must be dismissed as a general principle of psychology" (J. I. Downey, "Sexual Orientation and Psychoanalysis: Sexual Science and Clinical Practice." New York: Columbia University Press, 2002. P. 39).

Dr. Janet Cummings further noted, "The belief that homo- sexuality is always inbred flies in the face of available evidence that genetics, childhood environment, and personal choice are all factors. Granted, some may be more salient than others, but from the genetics standpoint alone, the genes responsible **would have disappeared throughout the millennial from lack of reproductive activity**" (Bold added). (F.S. Collins, "The Language of God. New York: Press, 2006. p. 260).

Camille Paglia, a lesbian activist, said, "There is an element of choice in all behavior, sexual or otherwise."

(C.Paglia, "Vamps and Tramps: New Essays. New York: Vintage Books, 1994. p.90.).

In 2000, the American Psychiatric Association was set to ban reorientation therapy. "Though skeptical, Spitzer conducted his research and was surprised at the results. He found that 66 percent of the men and 44 percent of the women had achieved good heterosexual functioning. That **reorientation therapy was successful in 89 percent of the men and 95 percent of the women,** both groups were bothered only slightly or not at all by unwanted homosexual attractions" (R.L. Spitzer, "Can

Some Gay Men and Lesbians Change from Homosexual to Heterosexual Orientation." Archives of Sexual Behavior, 32. No. 5. Oct. 2003. p. 403-17).

As of this date, there has been zero scientific evidence to prove same-sex attraction linked to DNA or any hereditary factor. Yes, zero evidence to prove the concept that one is born gay into this lifestyle.

Case studies conducted with monozygotic, (identical twins) do not support the records that same-sex attraction is a genetic trait. One twin may be involved in a homosexual lifestyle, while, at the same time, the other twin will live an ordinary heterosexual sexual life. If it were a genetic factor, 100% of the twins would both carry on in a same-sex lifestyle.

Next is the plain fact that it is possible, through effective counseling, for one to setback the bonds of this lifestyle and return to a productive heterosexual life. These are facts that hardcore communists, who promote this way of life, do not want society to recognize or accept. They strongly (even hatefully) do not wish society to consider the possibility of these facts being true. However, scientific evidence exists to prove this to be a straightforward statistic.

COMPASSION or LOVE

Those who support this alternative movement are very active in calling those who differ "people who are hateful, bigots, or homophobic" Those who respectfully disagree try to point out how this way of life is limiting both the individual and our society from achieving the utmost of what life has to offer. Consequently, we see increasing pressure from the political Communist activists who are forcing society to recognize this way of living as an acceptable lifestyle. Because of this recognition, those who have the feelings of living a substitute way of life are becoming less and less willing or likely to be aware of the fact they do not have to remain in this living arrangement.

As society is becoming more open to accepting this pattern of life, there are fewer reasons for a person to even try living their life by their gender-specific role. So the question is; which side is ensuring the greater benefit or most significant harm? Are the ones who support this movement showing a sincere compassion or love for those who follow this lifestyle? Instead, is it those who want to reach out and help them understand they can return to live their God-designed purpose here on earth?

Again the question lies before us: is it a valid form of empathy when citizens support others in falling away from their natural creation or is it truly a deeper caring love when trying to reach out and offer hope and assist one in fulfilling their God-given gender? What is the answer to the question, is it encouragement to draw closer to our Creator and deny Communist control or to impair one's eternal life and family by supporting Communism?

This homosexual movement is a freedom that is reaching way too deep into the lifeline of the family and our society. If we do not take a stance in facing up to its vulnerability, a larger percentage of individuals will fall into the deception of living this way, thereby depriving more and more individuals the opportunity of fulfilling their designed purpose to live a more rewarding and meaningful life.

By no longer yielding to the "fable of this communist substitute lifestyle", we will be reaching out to others when offering them an admirable ray of hope, to live a more productive and prosperous life during their time on this earth.

BATTLE for AGENCY

The question we need to ask is: Why is there this ongoing **battle for man's agency** and liberty versus Communism seeking for power over a man? Why the fight by men of influence to refuse man's right to his agency, his right to follow his political religion, to worship his God? Why? Moreover, when did it start to take hold in America?

Communist control in America took off as of the 1960s. America experienced civil disobedience with the Hippy movement, courts removing religious rights from schools, the inclusion of abortion rights, the insertion of the homosexual movement, no-fault divorce laws, creation of the welfare system, and with the assignation of President Kennedy.

If President John F. Kennedy would have been allowed to finish out his term as President he would have inhibited many of the Communist Goals. As a religious man, he would have restrained the introduction of the homosexual and civil disobedience movements. Kennedy was for lower taxes to create jobs and to bring the national debt back to balance. Last he drove Communist military influence out of our Western hemisphere with the Cuban Missile Crisis. President Kennedy was an enemy of Communism, and so was his brother Robert Kennedy, therefore, the Communist saw to it to have them both removed. At that point, World Communism gained full control of the Democratic Party.

To enhance the agenda of the Communist Democratic Party, they are working hard in using two powerful tools to gain control of the American voter, which are immigration and entitlements. These two tools are instrumental to direct the uninformed, misguided voters to follow the footsteps of their communist agenda of power over America.

The strategic reasons for immigration of Muslims follow up on Communist goal #22 discredit American culture, goal #29 to discredit the Constitution with their Sharia Law, and goal #17 to force acceptance and control through indoctrination in the school system. Read chapter 4 for more information on Muslims.

The main purpose of illegal immigration by the Democratic Party is to destroy the middle class, the poor Blacks, and Hispanics, and to overload the education system and break down the teaching of American history (goal #31). An additional concern over illegal immigration is the role of the Democratic Party and their support for Sanctuary Cities (goals #29 and #31). These concerns explicitly show the intent of the Democratic Party to defy and breakdown the Constitution by undermining the law and violating their oath of office.

Next their unlawful action is designed to overpower the national debt with entitlements for illegals and refugees while influencing them to register so they can vote for the Communist Democratic Party entitlement handouts. Entitlement programs are designed to destroy the character of the people and their family (goals #6, #29, #32). If entitlement programs are to exist, they should only be administered by the local community, not controlled by the federal government as intended by the Founding Fathers through the 10th Amendment. Local government always performs at a more efficient level for the citizens and tax payer.

Entitlements have been the greatest destruction of the Black race in America. Abortion was created as a means to diminish their birth rate. The Welfare program, as stated by President Johnson, was to enslave the "Negro's vote" for the Democrats for the next 200 years (goal #25).

Today 90% of Blacks vote for the Communist Democratic Party, and how have they benefited? The Black community is the poorest financial voters in America. They make up the highest percentage of unemployed. They receive the lowest annual income as citizens and are the slightest educated, and they have the most suppressed family with a 74% out of wedlock birth rate.

Members of Black organizations, such as "Black Lives Matter", unfortunately, are living in the footprints of political anarchy while encouraging a communist movement of breaking down the family.

The Guardian U.S. (New York international newspaper) reported on July 10, 2015, law enforcement killed 547 persons. Of the dead, 28.3% were Blacks who make up 13.2% of the population. Based on these figures the Black Lives Matter group wants America to believe Black cops and White cops look to kill Blacks openly. What about the facts reported 11/09/2015 titled "The Color of Crimes: Blacks are statistically 50 times more likely to attack Whites than vice versa." (http://www.newnation.org/NNN-Black-on-White.html).

The question we have the right to ask, "Who then is the real racist, Blacks or White people? Blacks kill their Black people 350% more than the Black or White police officers. Plus, they attack Whites 50 times more than Whites attack Blacks. Again who are the real racist people?

What is the truth? Let's look for the underlying reason for these statistics. The reason is clear, 74% of all Black babies will be born without a father. Blacks have the highest rate of school dropout setting the standard for achieving the lowest level of education compared to Hispanics or Whites. Blacks are at the highest level of unemployment in America.

Blacks took the lives of over 6000 Blacks in 2014. Law enforcement killed 154 black men who were in the act of committing a crime. Blacks murdered 6000 Blacks while the Black killer was in the act of a crime. Blacks will conduct crimes against Whites far more than their population percentage.

Underlining the real truth is something Backs do not want to recognize. The Black man is unwilling to accept the <u>responsibility of manhood and fatherhood</u> when causing a woman to become pregnant, not willing to marry the woman to take care of the child. A certain percentage of men will not receive the level of education required to develop career skills to support a family.

As a result, they have lost the sense of worth for who they are and what they are. They have created an atmosphere of social lowliness for the family of their doings not at the expense of Whites. They want to accuse Whites of their problems instead of looking for real solutions. Therefore, the number one problem is the man, not law enforcement. Until they are willing to accept what is happening, and while they still continue to vote for Democratic Communism, the Black race in America will continue to follow a complex life pattern in this country.

NOTE: It is to the advantage of the Democrat Party to keep people financially less well off, Obama's low rate of employment for minorities helps him at the voting polls. Communist understands people who are poor always vote for government entitlements believing they require the government to help them sustain a living.

It is unfortunate to say the Black man is following along with the Communist goal #40, "**Discredit the family as an institution**, encouraging promiscuity." Without a doubt, they are helping the Communist accomplish goals #22,25,31,32, and 41. We can only hope their acts will not bring about anarchy.

<u>WIN *FOR COMMUNISM.*</u>

That is a major problem both the Hispanic and the Blacks are facing today in America (Hispanic vote 67% and Blacks 90% for the Democratic Party). Unknowingly they vote for those who will not offer government policies to create jobs, for those who do not support Christianity, those who do not support family ethics, those who entice them to vote for entitlements that downgrade both the individual and the family. Constraining them to live at a lesser fulfilling life as they vote for communism.

Immigration: As stated earlier entitlements and immigration are essential tools used by today's Communist to break down, gain control, to take over America. The issue of illegal Hispanic immigration has become their most powerful and fundamental instrument to accomplish their goal.

Politically it is stated one of the major concerns for the Republican Party is the question of bringing about illegal immigration to a pathway to citizenship. However, the real issue is not the Republican Party it is the unawareness and misinformed Hispanic voters willingness to devastate America through their illegal immigration voting desires.

Today's Hispanic voters politically, morally, and by the lack of constitutional experience fail to understand immigration is for two reasons: first to protect jobs and second to protect the security of the country. If the voters continue to vote for the Democratic Party for the purpose to receive entitlements and/or flood America with unauthorized individuals, they need to understand:

1. They are playing in the hands of Communist to destroy America.
2. They will increasingly lose jobs to support their family.
3. Will decrease their ability to make a livable income.
4. Bring about greater poverty to America and themselves.
5. They will aid the Communist in destroying the middle class.
6. Will be responsible in abiding in destroying family values.
7. Increase gang activity, drug violence, and crime.
8. They will be discarding the right to religious freedom.
9. They will unconsciously be supporting a financial meltdown of America.
10. They will be giving up their future liberty.

When going to the polls, every voter needs to be aware what is truly going to take place for the individual, for the family, and for America when supporting communism in America.There are a right way and a wrong way to every issue. Currently, the Democrat Party's way to immigration is the wrong way.

YES, we need to improve our immigration policies, bring them to meet the needs of this country, but only in the way it is for the benefit of all people and for the sake of the USA no matter what country others may come from.

When thinking immigration, we must think America First then immigration. It is time to leave other flags behind and become an unhyphenated American. It is time for all citizens to put America first, before there is no longer an America, no longer The United States of America.

Please keep in mind when people rise out of poverty, there is no need for entitlements. By keeping people in poverty Communism increases their control, people grow in slavery.

Lenin understood that to control the people Communism must control:

Education	Healthcare	Property (taxation)
Religion	National Debt	Family

These are the long-term goals of today's Democratic Party Leadership in reaching out to accomplish the 45 objectives of Communist One World Oder.

WRAPPING UP

1. Russia has been infiltrating America since 1919.
2. Roosevelt, Clinton, and Obama have provided Russia and China with unlimited military power.
3. Obama's goal is to support and strength of world Communism.
4. The Democratic Party is following the 45 Communist Goals to take over America.
5. The dictatorial objectives of the Communist Party are to destroy the Christian Religion, the **Family**, and the Constitution.

6. Communist leaders conclude the only way they could finally impose their totalitarian will over the West was first by **taking over its education, and then religion.**
7. Each American has a national debt responsibility of $56,604,000. This is building up communist countries who cry DEATH TO AMERICA.
8. Since 1960, World Communism controls the Democrats.
9. NEA - controlled by Communist organizations.
10. Courts are controlling Religious Expression in America.
11. World Christian Council (WCC) has been infiltrated by the Communist.
12. Education, social agencies, and welfare programs are being directed by the Communist Democratic Party to control America.
13. Communism emphasizes the need to raise children away from the influence of parents.
14. Communism wants to discredit our Founding Fathers and the Exceptionalism of America.
15. Divorce, abortion, and homosexuality are critical programs of the Communists.
16. With a **vote of 5,854 to 3,810,** homosexuality was eliminated, as a diagnosis category from the psychiatric manual.
17. Homosexuality is an emotional disorder.
18. "Dr. Spitzer concludes that homosexuality is not invariably Fixed."
19. There is zero scientific evidence to prove same-sex attraction is linked to DNA or hereditary factors.
20. Entitlement programs end up destroying the character of the individual and their family.
21. The communist goal is to destroy the middle class. In 1970, 61% of the households were classified as middle class, today, 2015, only 50%.
22. Today 90% of the Blacks vote for the Communist Democrats.
23. Karl Marx stated that for his communist revolution to come about; it would require abolishing the traditional family.

CHAPTER 4

—§—

Islam Is A Communist Political Religion

Islam: Communist ideology, lacking moral equivalency in principles of freedom, America, and Christianity.

PHIL CLARK

ACCORDING TO PEW Research Center as of 2010, Christianity was the world's largest religion with an estimated 2.2 billion followers representing nearly a third (31 percent) of all 6.9 billion people on Earth. Islam had 1.6 billion followers representing 23 percent of the global population.

However, Pew Research projects in 2050 the Muslim population will increase by 73 percent being 30 percent of the world's population (2.8 billion). Christians will make up 31 percent of the population (2.9 billion). By 2070, Pew Research believes the number of Muslims will globally surpass Christians. (http://www.pewforum.org/2015/04/02/religious-projections-2010-2050/pf_15-04-02_projectionstables8/).

Another factor to consider as of 2010 is that more than a quarter of the world's total population was under the age of 15. The highest percentage of children younger than 15 years belong to the Muslim population, which made up 34 percent compared to Hindus at 30 percent and Christians at 27 percent. (http://www.people-press.org/2011/08/30/section-1-a-demographic-portrait-of-muslim-americans/).

The world is going through tremendous changes in many ways. However, the most important warning for society to consider is the direction of the

Religious Political projection for the world. Again there are only two kinds of Political Religions in the world. One religion is of Man (Ex: Islam) and the second is of God, Jesus Christ, the creator of this earth.

Unfortunately, there is an ongoing conflict as to who is the creator of this earth. Christians believe the Creator is Jesus Christ (God of the Bible), the Jews believe His name to be YHWH (God of the Torah), and Muslims believe it to be Allah (moon god of the Quran).

Currently, all world terrorism and large-scale killings are being sponsored by only one Political Religion that being Islam. Terrorist have killed almost 33,000 people in 2014.

(http://www.vocativ.com/news/203660/terrorists-killed-almost-33000-people-around-the-world-last-year/).

Christians and Jews are voluntarily in harmony with today's world. However, Islam lacks in fulfilling the humanitarian needs of the world by taking an entirely different position in the rigorous Political debate.

Within the Christian and Jewish faiths, they are very straight forward in their relationship with all nations and with the individual. They submit that individuals have the right to select how they want to live, only asking that people of faith are allowed their beliefs.

However, Islam is not so simple as they give the appearance of being divided into positions within their own Political Religion. One side claims to represent a people of peace, and one side's (Muslim Brotherhood) actions are not of peace but of a totalitarian government.

Worldwide Israel is not trying to force other nations to live by their Political Religious beliefs. They are only endeavoring to defend God's covenant, and the land as approved by the U.N. for their existence. In fact, within the nation of Israel, Jewish people allow all Muslims the right to practice their faith without fear of judgment.

As for Christian nations, they enter Muslim countries only with the desire to provide freedom of agency and liberty from the totalitarian Muslim Brotherhood. Christians are offering their blood and resources to protect those individuals forced into submission by the Muslim Brotherhood.

In opposition to and in defiance of man's liberty, the Muslim Brotherhood cannot point to a single nation or people at any time in history where Islam is willing to sacrifice their lives and money to defend the rights of the population. Throughout history, Muslims have proven only to take control, destroy nations, and the agency of the people. They share no history of defending society, no history of compassion for a nation. This statement is <u>absolutely</u> 100% correct, without question or any form of exception.

The Brotherhood forces the ideology that one either believes the way they want a person to believe or they will cut off his head, which they have been doing to Christians by the thousands. The Brotherhood terrorizes a country while those who cry out "we are of peace" are outrageously standing by doing nothing to defend the right of humanity. Just what kind of a god do these people follow? It appears they follow a god, who will not protect or respect life and liberty for humanity.

Some may choose to say this is not an honest, fair, or truthful statement. They may say the Brotherhood being much better financed, with military support, are so overpowering there is no way the current members of Islam can defend and overwhelm the Brotherhood.

Let's remind members of Islam to look back to the year of 1776, a time in history when God-fearing men of America took on the most powerful nation in the world. Americans were substantially underfunded and without the proper required military support. However, with faith and reliance upon God they won their liberty and became the greatest nation on earth. So do not tell us that it cannot be accomplished overtaking the Brotherhood. Islam just needs to have the desire, courage, and faith in God to fight for humanity. The question remains "what and where is your faith in Allah"? Does Allah believe in liberty? Islam's actions will stand as a witness to these issues.

A reasonable and honest answer to the question was provided by Brigitte Gabriel in a panel discussion about Benghazi. A Muslim lady posed the question, why associate all Muslims with the attacks on America when the majority of Muslims are peaceful? (https://www.youtube.com/watch?v=o7fBqlyjESg)

Brigitte pointed out how that statement was irrelevant. She went on to say that Hitler started WW II and killed 6 million Jews. Russia and China killed 100's of millions of citizens, and the vast majority of the Germans, Russians, and Chinese people were all peaceful. Just like Islam today, they stood by and did nothing to stop the killing of innocent human beings. Those supposed peaceful citizens are irrelevant. That is precisely the current position of the supposedly good peaceful citizens of Islam. They just sit by and allow millions of innocent individuals to be slaughtered by the Muslim Brotherhood. Again, what kind of god and people will allow this to take place? When considering the principles of compassion for our fellow men what kind of god does Islam follow? Please stand up and answer the question.

If "sincere, peaceful members of Islam" will not respond to the above affairs, then it is the responsibility of the world to answer these questions for them.

RELIGIOUS PERSONALITIES

When talking about any form of Political Religion we first need to acknowledge that the members of that Political Religion will consist of many different personalities and degrees of personal commitments towards their Political Religion organization. They are members either because of their birth, peer group association, or their intellectual environment.

Some Islamic followers may believe in, or be willing to support this religion to a limited degree eventually showing signs of inactivity. They are weak in principles and very non-committal social-economically to Islam. In essence, they wish to bother no one, while willing to sit on the sidelines. We refer to this person as a Sleeper.

Next there are those who are very sincere in their belief. They are honest and practice a willingness to allow others to live by their choosing without a commitment to their way of life. This person is known as a

Hearten. Last are the Wolves in sheep's clothing, who wear their Political Religion with hardening and controlling designs. Their Political Religion is the only correct way; others must accept their beliefs or pay the consequences. These are called Wolves or Harden members, the Brotherhood. They are very dangerous servants for humanity and will do whatever it takes to gain power, money, social influence, and control. The real meaning of truth and liberty is not important to them. They only want to force others to follow their designs for the world.

Today's Islamic people are a composite of these three kinds of personalities. The problem the world faces is that, as Brigitte Gabriel would say, the Muslims Sleepers and Hearten are irrelevant to the Wolves/Harden members of Islam. No matter what the feelings or desires are of the Sleepers and Hearten the Wolves/Harden (Muslim Brotherhood) control Islam with full authority and design. They are using their stratagem and power in creating a totalitarian Communist World.

Islam is a Communist Political Religion because they <u>do not allow for free agency of man.</u> They do follow a god but just what kind of a god is he? Where does this god reside? What is his purpose for the world? Based on his ruling authority, it is impossible the god of Islam is or can be the creator of this earth because their god does not show compassion and tenderness. Their god supports degrees of murder and rape. Their god is about control, not agency. Their god places the woman in a lower state, not as an equal heir. Their god lacks integrity when authorizing one to lie. Their god promotes war, not peace. Their god has never liberated individuals or a nation who may be under political oppression. This god is not the kind of god who created the earth. Their god is a god, who lives by the rules of Communism and Nazism political religions.

Of course, the Sleepers and Hearten will cry out no "we are for peace". We do not support the Brotherhood. We are not like them. They do not follow the prophet, Muhammad. We do, we believe in freedom of all humanity." Sorry, Sleepers and Hearten, the world, wants an Islam, who walks the talk not just talks the talk. Until Islam is willing to show the world they will correct the destructive behavior of their

Brotherhood, there is no need to accept Islam as a worthy or honest government.

The Presuppositions of Islam (based on the idea that something is true or will happen).

Islam presents several concepts to support Muhammad as a prophet. They believe that Islam is the one and only true religion upon the earth. Six Islamic presuppositions are:

A. Muhammad was a prophet.
B. Muhammad was a direct descendant of Abraham.
C. Today's Quran is the single source of the words of Allah.
D. Denial that Christ is the Son of God and that Christ did not die on the cross.
E. Christians and Jews have corrupted the Bible, the word of God, to support their gospel position.
F. Sharia Law is Muhammad's words.

A. Muhammad a Prophet

Muhammad was born 570 A.D. as a member of the Quraysh tribe. Tragedy hit Muhammad early in his life with the death of both parents. Besides the unfortunate consequences of losing his parents, Muhammad was subject to mental and emotional distractions of epileptic seizures. As an example, Muhammad one day fell to the ground from an epileptic seizure and cried out that demons were cutting open his stomach to steal something from his body. Throughout his life, those surrounding him believed there were times Muhammad was under the influence of demons. "Muhammad did experience hallucinations and delusions within his life."

(https://kjvbiblebveliever.wordpress.com/2013/07/22/muhammads- demon-he-originally-thought-he-was-possessed/).

Epilepsy is a central system disorder (neurological disorder). Nerve cell activity in the brain becomes sensations and sometimes causes loss of consciousness. As of today, there is no known cure for Epilepsy. It was an emotional condition Muhammad suffered throughout his lifetime followed by hallucinations and delusions. There are those of the medical field in studying about the life of Muhammad who have commented on his mental state:

"Depicting a psychological profile of Mohammad has been, because of the Quran's many mistakes, incomprehensible verses, contradictions, inconsistencies, fallacies, errors, and absurdities, a central issue for those who have been researching on Islam. As examples, I mention two classic scholars: Aloy Sprenger, in his fascinating three-volume work about Mohammad and Islam (Das Leben und die Lehre des Muhammed), categorizes Mohammad as having **suffered from hysteria**.

"In recent years, Ali Sina is the only one I know who has performed comprehensive research about Mohammad's psychological makeup... Muhammad may have also suffered from schizophrenia. He attributes all the **hallucinations and delusions** Muhammad experienced to his Temporal Lobe epilepsy." (http://en.europenews.dk/A-psychopatholog-ical-profile-of-the-prophet-Mohammad-Part-1-of-5-78166.html).   (Bold added).

The valid question is, what might Muhammad's followers say about his mental state, those who lived with him as written in the Quran? Moreover, they say: "O you (Muhammad) to whom the Dhikr (the Qur'an) has been sent down! Verily, you are a **madman**. Why do you not bring angels to us if you are of the truthful ones?" (S. 15:6 Hilali-Khan). Good questions, a madman with no angels?

"Then they had turned away from him (Messenger Muhammad) and said: "One (Muhammad) taught (by a human being), a madman!" (S. 44:14 Hilali-Khan; cf. Q. 34:46; 37:36; 68:2, 51). OK, a madman! Not taught by a divine source but by a human being.

However, they turned away from him, saying, "Well educated, but crazy!" (44:14) Again a madman **or crazy**! (Bolding Added).

Without question, Muhammad lived the life as a mentally troubled man. That is a critical condition the world needs to understand, a condition that <u>disqualifies his credibility as a prophet.</u>

At the age of 12, he visited Syria for his first exposure to Jews and Christian's ideology. While Muhammad was in Syria, he developed respect for their religions. This connection came about from listening to the teachings of the Books of the Bible, not by personal education for Muhammad was an <u>illiterate man</u>, an oddity that no Bible prophet ever exemplified.

At age 25 Muhammad married Khadija, who was his employer and older at the age of 40. Khadija was of the Jewish faith, and thereby their marriage took place in the Jewish tradition. Moreover, Khadija's faith influenced Muhammad in the knowledge of religion stemming from her Jewish background.

During a time of uncertainty in Muhammad's life, as a troubled man (age 40+) he took refuge in a cave at the foot of Mount Hira. It is there he states he received his first vision from the angel Gabriel. He was instructed to "arise and warn" the world about the false gods and spread the divine message from Allah. Allah is the ancient name for "Moon God".

The angel Gabriel is well known by the Jewish and Christian faiths as a messenger from God. The angel Gabriel appeared to both Zechariah, the father of John the Baptist, John being a forerunner of Jesus Chris, and to Mary, the mother of Jesus Christ. Gabriel informed Zechariah of the coming of his son John when saying "I stand in the presence of God, and I have been sent to speak to you and to tell you this good news." (Luke 1:19). Later Gabriel appeared to Mary (Luke 1:30-31) "And the angel said unto her, Fear not, Mary: for thou hast found favor with God...behold, thou shalt conceive in thy womb, and bring forth a son, and shalt call his name JESUS."

Gabriel visited other prophets such as Daniel and Moses. Each time he was a divine messenger sent from God the Father to represent Jesus Christ as the Son of God, the Savior, and Creator of the world. The Bible has recorded 70+ messengers sent from Heaven to prophets to prepare the way of the coming Savior. At no time in biblical history did Gabriel ever represent someone with the attributes and personality as possessed by the god of Islam.

Islam tells the world that it was Gabriel, who visited Muhammad in the cave on behalf of Allah. However, that is not a possibility. Gabriel could not have taught Muhammad of as he was not capable of instructing him of any god called Allah. Jesus Christ is the sole purpose and mission of Gabriel. Such a god as Allah is an unknown to the mission and life of Gabriel.

At this point, Muhammad proclaims **himself** to be a prophet, a **self-proclaimed prophet,** which no other Bible prophet was capable of declaring. He is not able to offer sustaining evidence of this divine intervention; there are no historical facts to support his claim. After sharing his experience with his wife, it was Khadija, not Muhammad, to suggest he might be a prophet.

Shortly after announcing his position as a prophet Muhammad then transformed into a military warrior. It began when attacking non-threating caravans of innocent people, and stealing their wealth. It is believed Muhammad orchestrated 60+ battles while personally leading some 27 battles. Most battles ended in capturing property, rape of women, slavery, and murder. In celebration of victory, contraband was taken, women were turned over to his men to do as they wished to, rape or enslave or both. Often, their husbands had their heads cut off.

One historic battle reported by Ishaq Sirat Rasul Allah relates an incident on how Muhammad beheaded Jewish men at the battle of Banu Qurayza. "Three Jewish tribes rejected Mohammad and his teachings. He responded by exiling two of the tribes while exercising severe judgment against the third one. He called for every man in the tribe to be beheaded (600–900 men), and his followers were to take the women, children, and property for a personal reward". (A Biblical Point of View on Islam by Kerby Anderson, 2007, p 15–16).

Today's Islamic Brotherhood is adverse to freedom of speech, the right to express opposition to Islam. Even Muhammad assassinated those who spoke out against him.

The first person whom he assassinated was an elderly Jewish man. Muhammad asked, "Who will rid me of Ibnu' l Ashraf?" One of his followers responded, "I will deal with him for you. O Apostle of God, I will kill him." Muhammad gave his blessing, but later his follower returned to Muhammad and said to kill this man, he would have to lie. Again, Muhammad gave his followers his blessing. So this follower and a few other Muslims tricked the man into leaving his house so they could kill him with daggers, and swords."

The account concludes with the statement that "our attack upon God's enemy cast terror among the Jews, and there was no Jew in Median who did not fear for his life."

(http://www.answering-islam.org/Silas/ashraf.htm).

Not only did Muhammad require those who spoke against him to be assassinated, but he also authorized men to lie in accomplishing his wishes. Lying in Islam is allowed under the ruling of **al-Taqiyya:** "Muslims lie not because they are liars by nature but by choice. Systematic lying as a religious policy is deadly, and if our politicians do not understand this, thousands could and will die.

"Muslims lie when it is in their interest to do so and "Allah" will not hold them accountable for lying when it is beneficial to the cause of Islam. They can lie without any guilt or fear of accountability or retribution. A lie in the defense of Islam is approved even applauded in their "holy" books." (http://muslimfact.com/bm/terror-in-the-name-of-islam/islam-permits-lying-to-deceive-unbelievers-and-bri.shtml).

One embarrassing event in Muhammad's life is when he said Satan put words in his mouth. (Read the website http://www.666soon.com/who_was_ muhammad.htm, the article titled "Who was Muhammad?). States: "Not able to protect his remaining followers, Muhammad compromised with the Mecca's by incorporating some of their idols into the evolving religion of Islam. He proclaimed that Al-Lat, Al-Uzza, and Manat, three Mecca deities, were exalted goddesses, and their intercession were to be sought. This led to Mecca's accepting Islam, but Muhammad later had to confess that Satan inspired the compromise." (www.contender-ministries.org/islam/muhammad.php).

If Muhammad openly admits to being inspired by Satan, when dealing with the people of Mecca, it is very reasonable to believe he was inspired by Satan and not by Gabriel during his visit to the cave. Satan has a history of deceiving man. Starting with Cain in the Old Testament and following in the New Testament of a man overcome by 1,000 Devils. Mentally weak persons, like Muhammad, have easily been **controlled** by bad spirits.

How is it, as a prophet of God, he would even consider compromising on pagan issues such as the idea that they "were exalted goddesses, and their intercession was to be sought," and to do so solely for **political gain**? It is not within the credibility of a prophet to take such a false position.

Islam tells the world that Allah is the same god as of the Bible. How can that be? Based on the common sense of the Scriptures this is impossible. The laws of Allah are totally incompatible with the Bible. If Allah is not the god of the Bible then who was Muhammad's visitor? It could not have been Gabriel. Then what or who appeared to Muhammad? Did someone visit Muhammad? If so whom does the god of Islam represent?

It is time to examine the word "God". Webster's dictionary (1984 edition page 578) states:

"Any of various beings **<u>conceived</u>** of as supernatural, immortal, and having special powers over the lives and affairs of people and the course of nature." (Bold and underlining added)

Webster's online states:

"A spirit of being that has great power; strength, knowledge, and that can affect nature and the lives of people: one of various spirits or beings worshiped in some religions." Both definitions share the awareness of God's ability to affect lives, affairs, and course of nature.

Undeniably the God of the Jewish and Christian faith has generated, throughout the Bible, the ability to change lives, affairs of man, and of the course of nature (ex: Moses parting the sea, Jesus raising the dead and turning water to wine). However, the god of Islam, in the Quran, does change lives but does not show the same capability or humility as the God of the Bible to generate actions affecting man and the course of nature of proportionate response or ability. Therefore, it is reasonable to believe the God of the Bible, and the god of the Quran are separate and distinct individual personalities. They are not well-suited with one another. They are not of the same Religious Political creed as the leaders of Islam proclaim.

Unfortunately, it appears the god of Islam offers fewer qualifications to be the God of the Bible. The Bible and its prophets are not on the same wavelength as with the character and behavior of Islam.

B. Was Muhammad a direct descendant of Abraham?

Dr. Rafat Amari of the Religion Research Institute engaged in a 20-year full-time study of the history of Arabia, Islam, and Mecca. His first language is Arabic, and his study included source material in the Middle East. Dr. Rafat Amari has published the book "Islam: In Light of History."

In an article by Dr. Rafat Amari, "IS MOHAMMED A DESCENDENT OF ISHMAEL?" He states it is most unlikely that Muhammad could be a decedent of Ishmael based on historical archives for the following reasons:

1. Muslims believe Muhammad is a descendant of Ishmael based on genealogies written around 770 A.D.
2. They claim Muhammad was of the tribe of Nebaioth. These tribes disappeared after the 7th century B.C. approximately 12-13 centuries before the birth of Muhammad.
3. Muhammad's family is not connected to any Ishmaelite tribe. Muhammad's family did not leave Yemen until the 5th century A.D., 1,100 years after the Ishmaelite's disappeared.
4. Genealogy fabricated by Ibn-Ishak contradicts Muhammad, who expressed his ignorance about his ancestors prior to his 17th ancestor.
5. History proves **Muhammad was not a descendant of Ishmael.** For more information read: (http://religionresearchinstitute.org/mohammad/ishmael.htmhttp://www.historyofmecca.com/origins_of_islam.htm).

CURRENT QURAN IS THE SINGLE SOURCE OF THE WORD OF ALLAH.

1. Islam claims the Quran is the word of god Allah. Therefore, the world has the right to expect that the Quran is 100% accurate. However, Historians and scholars have found that is not the case. There is such a wide variety of discrepancies and contradictions in the Quran. Researchers have found that the Quran consist of <u>255 contradictions</u>. In one Surah, god says one thing. Then in another Surah god contradicts himself; (Example: "In Surah 2:256 God tells Muhammad not to impose Islam by force, "There is no compulsion in religion," Then in verse 193 He tells his messenger to kill whoever rejects Islam." The Quran also states incorrect scientific and mathematical facts. The time frame of events and customs is misplaced. (For more information visit the internet under Quran discrepancies and contradictions for validation).

2. Those who supposedly wrote the Quran were 3rd and 4th hand accounts, *non-inspired men* (as in the Bible), are written some 150 years after the death of Muhammad. The Quran was memorized by individuals. However, they did not come together to write them down or put them in book form. "Those passages had not been written down, and following the death of those who knew them, they were no longer available but lost forever; nor had Abu Bakr, nor Umar nor Uthman as of yet collected the text of the Quran." (The True Guidance, An Introduction To Qur'anic Studies, part 4 (Light of Life – PO Box 13, A-9503 Villach, Austria, p. 47 citing Ibn Kathir's Al-Bidaya wa al-Nibaya, chapter on the Battle of Yamama).

3. Zuhri reports, "During the battle of Yamama (632 A.D.), 450 reciters of the Quran perished." (Ibid). Original sources were no longer available to write the Quran.

4. "Muslims often claim that the manuscript of the Quran housed in the Topkapi Museum in Istanbul, Turkey is one of the oldest sources. Muslims say it dates from around 650 A.D. There is an insurmountable problem with this. This document is written in

Kufic (also known as *al-Khatt al-Kufi)* script. Coins in the British Museum show that the first coins using the Kufic script date from the mid to end of the 8th century. The only script used during and after Muhammad's days was the *Jazm* script". (http://www.bibleprobe.com/corruptedquran.htm).

5. "The Samarkand (aka Othman Koran) manuscript in the Soviet Library in Tashkent, Uzbekistan also uses the Kufic script, indicating late 8th century. Many believe it is the oldest in existence. Only About one-third of the original survives." (Ibid).

6. The Nairaland Formun reports there are five versions of the Quran: Transmitter Hafs, Duuri, Warsh, Suusi, and Qaaluum.

> It is reported: "Hudhaifa was afraid of their differences in Recitation of the Quran...Uthman sent to every Muslim province one copy of what they had copied and ordered that all other Quran materials, whether written in fragmentary manuscript or whole copies, be burnt." (Hadith, Vol. 6, Book 61, #510). Uthman is saying it is OK to burn the word of God, <u>and Uthman is the one to decide just what should be in the book.</u> (http://www.bible.ca/islam/islam-quran-changed-editing-process.htm). "The Sana'a Qur'an find of 1972. Workers, restoring a mosque in Sana'a, Yemen, stumbled across a cache of Qur'an manuscripts in the structure of the building's roof. It was not until 1997 that 35,000 microfilm images of the documents were finally allowed to leave the country so others could examine the materials. This find also gives evidence of variation from today's Qur'an in both the reading of the text and its order, something unthinkable in traditional Islamic doctrine." (Ibid).

7. It is reasonable to find copies of the Quran written in different forms. The problem is that of Islam's erroneously claim there is only one version making the Quran the purest of scriptures. Agan Islam was entrenched in lying to protect a pseudo-Religious government.

C. Denial that Christ is the Son of God and He did not die on the cross.

One of the greatest deceptions stated by Islam is that Christ did not die on the cross and was not resurrected. This statement, without question, is so ignorantly blatant and so quickly to confirm. Only a foolish man would even try to falsify such a historical event as the death and resurrection of Jesus Christ.

First, the world has the first-hand witness written by four apostles, Mark, Matthew, John, and Luke. This has been historically verified over and over for the last 2,000 years?

Next, our dating system of B.C. and A. D. has not been challenged over the centuries in honor of Christ's birth.

There are five well-known Academic scholars and historians of the 1st-century source (not a150 years later) who have written (testified) as to the truthfulness of this event. They are Tacitus (109 A.D.), "Ammals" chapter 44 states: "Christus, the founder of the name, put to death by Pontius Pilate." Flavius Josephus (37 A.D. – 100 A.D.), the Roman historian, wrote of the death and resurrection of Jesus in the book "Antiquities," written 93-94 AD. Next, there was Suetonius (69-122 A.D.) works, "Life of the Emperor Claudius" states – they "worship the crucified sage, and live after his law." We have Piny the Elder (77 A.D.), who wrote about Jesus' death in the "Book X of his Epistles." Later we find Julius Africanus quoting Thallus (52 A.D.19 years after Christ's crucifixion) a Roman historian, who wrote "On the whole world here pressed a most fearful darkness and the rocks were rent by an earthquake, and many places in Judea and other districts were thrown down." Thallus' writings are in complete compliance with the gospel as written by Mark, Matthew, Luke, and John.

Christ was crucified around 33 A.D. thereby placing the Roman historians living at the time of the death of Christ as close second source historians making them a **far more reliable** source and during a more definite tie period than the writings of the Quran.

So who is the person and when did certain events take place that authorized Islam to lie outright about Christ's death on the cross and of His resurrection?

D. Christians and Jews have corrupted the Bible, the word of God, to support their position.

Again like Communists, they make a statement without supporting evidence. Islam does not provide historical facts to show the Bible has been corrupted to support the Jewish or Christian beliefs.

"The truth is the Christian Bible can be nearly reconstructed today from the 24,800 copies of original manuscripts still in existence and the 80,000 quotations from early church fathers. Also, many people who walked and talked with Jesus wrote to us about His life. The Christian Gospels are so widely distributed that any attempt to change (add/subtract) they would have resulted in the immediate discovery." In fact, the Qur'an attests to the validity of the Christian Gospels and the Torah. Jewish scribes painstakingly copied the Torah via a system of checking, double checking and adding each letter on each line. Any attempt to change something in the Torah would have resulted in the sudden discovery." (http://www.bibleprobe.com/corruptedquran.htmen corrupted).

Surah 29: 46- "And dispute ye not with the people of the scriptures of the Book, but say, "We believe in the revelation which has come down to us and in that which came down to you: Our Allah and your Allah is one." Allah told Mohammad not to question the scriptures of the Christians." Later Muhammad is known to use the Torah as a legal document: (Underling added).

Again, Islam is caught telling another lie which is true to their character.

RULES OF THE PROPHETS

Let's review some of the guidings norms required of a Prophet.

Rules of a Prophet	Muhammad	Bible Prophets	Christ
Will not lie	did lie	yes	yes
Will not murder	did murder	yes	yes
Will not steal	did steal	yes	yes
Will not rape	did rape	yes	yes

Perform miracles	no	yes	yes
Heal the sick	no	yes	yes
Control of nature	no	yes	yes
Raise the dead	no	yes	yes
Allow freedom	no	yes	yes
Women rights	no	yes	yes

When discussing the governing rules of a prophet it appears Muhammad does not match up with the Bible or past Prophets. Based on Biblical scripture and historical facts, Muhammad lacks in moral equivalency. Please explain just how does Muhammad fit into the Bible or fit with the real God of the Bible?

E. Sharia Law vs. the Constitution

For Americans, their rule of law is based on the United States Constitution, but for Islam, their statute of law is based on Sharia Law.

Sharia Law may be described as the Islamic law, a complex system of ethical codes that govern all aspects of Muslim life.

More than merely "law," it is Islam's methodology through which Muslims engage their daily actions in search of divine guidance. For devout Muslims, Sharia Law governs everything they do from the way they eat, treat animals, protect the environment, do business, get married, distribute their estate after death, and do legal judgments.

Because of the many concerns with Sharia Law authorized as a form of law allowed within our court system, individual states are setting standards where foreign law shall have no consideration in place of our constitution.

For those who closely follow America's Constitution, their reasons for not sanctioning the use of Sharia Law in our court system is because they understand Sharia Law is in direct conflict with the Constitution as follows:

• <u>Amendment 1–Freedom of Religion, Press, Expression</u>

- <u>Amendment 5–Trial and Punishment, Compensation</u>
- <u>Amendment 6–Right to Speedy Trial, Confrontation of Witnesses</u>
- <u>Amendment 7–Trial by Jury in Civil Cases</u>
- <u>Amendment 8–Cruel and Unusual Punishment</u>
- <u>Amendment 10–Powers of the States and People</u>
- <u>Amendment 11–Judicial Limits</u>
- <u>Amendment 13–Slavery Abolished</u>
- <u>Amendment 14–Citizenship Rights</u>
- <u>Amendment 15–Race No Bar to Vote</u>
- <u>Amendment 19–Women's Suffrage</u>

Those in America, who engage with human rights issues of Sharia Law, point to reports such as the following by Paul Strand, a CBN News Washington Sr. Correspondent: "Activists Warn US Women of Sharia Law Threat," Sunday, May 13, 2012:

"Women who come from Muslim countries and share their experiences of living under Muslim laws tell us how Sharia's treatment of women is both 'oppressive' and 'violent.'

"Sharia Law does not identify women as citizens. And some jurists in Sharia law do not identify women as human beings. Some jurists would go so far as defining them as livestock. Once in America, they are free to talk about the stifling effect Sharia law would have on their unalienable rights of life, liberty, and the pursuit of happiness if allowed to be law in America.

"Women living under Sharia law are often in polygamous marriages; often in marriages where they do not have the freedom to pursue their education or pursue a career if that should interest them.

"It is estimated that as many as 5,000 Muslim women die in honor killings every year, which Islamic extremists declare imperative."

In an article by Laurie Roth (2012) titled "Sharia Law must be outlawed in the U.S." (Retrieved from http://www. renewamerica.com/columns/roth/121026), she states:

"Just some of the core values taught and enforced worldwide with Sharia Law include the following, which I have screamed about for years on my show and in other articles:

- Those converting to another faith should be executed.
- Islamic husbands can beat and rape their wives, marry many women, then divorce anyone of them for any reason. The wife cannot get out of her situation. She is trapped.
- Gays are to be executed.
- Rape victims are to be stoned if they do not have four supporting witnesses.
- Sharia Law supports beatings and dismem- bering of body parts for a variety of offenses, including stealing.
- You are to be killed if you criticize the prophet, Mohammed."

Then there are some who say, "That will never happen in America." For those who want to think that is true, maybe they should read the ar- ticle, "40 Percent of U.S. Muslim Voters Want Islamic Law, 12 Percent Want Death for Blasphemers" by Daniel Greenfield (2012):

"The poll also found 40 percent of Muslims in America believe they should not be judged by U.S. law and the Constitution, but by Shariah standards."

"Even more shocking: One in eight respondents said they think those Americans who criticize or parody Islam should face the death penalty." (Retrieved from http://frontpagemag.com/2012/dgreenfield/40-percent-of-us-muslim-voters-want-Islamic).

Again, for those who want to believe that Islam and Sharia law will have no effect on them, then let's take a look at what Ayesha Ahmed (2004) discovered in the article, "Sharia in America":

"Omar M. Ahmad founder of CAIR said: "Islam isn't in America to be equal to any other faith, but to become dominant," he said. "The Koran, the Muslim book of scripture, should be the highest authority in America, and Islam the only accepted religion on Earth," he said.

"Sharia Law does not grant the same rights for woman as for the man in several important instances, including marital and inheritance laws."

(Retrieved from http://www. cbsnews.com/8601-503544_162-20019405. HTML?assetTypeId=41&blogId=5).

<u>"Most people in Hell are women, and most women will go to Hell</u>

Ibn Abbas reported that Allah's Messenger (may peace be upon him) said: "I had a chance to look into the Paradise, and I found that majority of the people were poor, and I looked into the Fire, and there I found the majority constituted by women."

Sahih Muslim 36:6597, See Also Sahih Muslim 36:6598, Sahih Muslim 36:6599. (Underlining added).

<u>"Men have authority over women because God has made the one superior</u> to the other and because they spend their wealth to maintain them. Good women are obedient. They guard their unseen parts because God has guarded them. As for those whom you <u>fear disobedience</u>, <u>admonish them</u> and send them to beds apart and <u>beat them</u>. Then if they obey you, take no further action against them. Surely God is most high. "Qur'an 4:34. (Underlining added).

"While defending the status quo in legislatures, **Sharia law** has been advancing in other American institutions, including the following:

- An increasing number of American public schools with Muslim students are holding Islamic prayers towards Mecca while American public universities continue to build Muslim-only washing facilities. In 2013, Skokie School District 68 in Illinois became the first US school district to celebrate Eid al-Adha, a Muslim holy day, as a school holiday, instead of Veterans Day.

In 2014, Rocky Mountain High School in Fort Collins, Colorado, became the first high school to recite the Pledge of Allegiance in Arabic, replacing "One nation under God," with "One nation under Allah."

- In 1996, Bill Clinton became the first US president to hold an Eid al-Fitr dinner at the White House to celebrate the end of Ramadan, the Muslim month-long dawn-to-dusk fast. Eid al-Fitr includes six "Takbirs," the raising of hands and shouting, "Allahu Akbar!" to declare that **Allah, the moon god**, is the "Greatest."

- In 2000, the Republican National Convention became the first US presidential convention to open with a Muslim prayer to **Allah, the moon god**.

- In 2007, **Quran** for the first time was used to swear into office a new US Congressman, Keith Ellison.

- In 2009, Hudson County Superior Court Judge Joseph Charles Jr. ruled in S.D. v. M.J.R, that the Muslim ex-husband repeatedly had sexually assaulted his Muslim ex-wife, both before and after their divorce. Following testimony from the Muslim man's, imam, however, the judge denied the ex-wife's request for a permanent restraining order against her ex-husband, citing the Muslim man's "belief" and "practices": *"The court believes that [defendant] was operating under his belief that it is, as the husband, his desire to have sex when and whether he wanted to, was something that was consistent with his practices."*

- In 2009, a Christian US soldier at Baghram Air Force Base in Afghanistan received Bibles in two local languages sent by his American church as planned. The US military confiscated those Bibles and instead of at least returning them to the church, burned them. By contrast, when Terry Jones, a pastor in Florida, announced his plan to burn a copy of the **Quran** in 2010, General David Petraeus, the commander of the US military in Afghanistan, publicly objected to his plan, while US Secretary of State Hillary Clinton denounced his plan as "disgraceful."

- To attract and manage (Middle Eastern) Muslim wealth, an increasing number of American financial institutions are becoming Sharia-compliant. Requires donating a percentage of their annual profits to Islamic organizations designated by their Sharia-compliance advisors, many of whom are members of the **Muslim Brotherhood** and funnel money to even terrorist groups (donations must go to one or more of eight recipient categories, one of which is Jihad).
- Muslim taxi drivers are challenging local authorities for the right to refuse to pick up blind passengers with seeing-eye dogs while Muslim supermarket cashiers are challenging their employers for the right to refuse to sell products from pigs. Both are considered unclean in Islam." (http://www.billionbibles.org/sharia/america-sharia-law.html), (Underlining and bolding added).

Yes, only a few statements are listed above suggesting that Sharia law is very much counter to the principles of democracy and the American way of life. However, there are hundreds of such quotes by the political leaders of Islam. The reason is that Islam and their Sharia law is not in harmony with the nature of democracy. It is a politically forced standard of living under the name of religion: a Doctrinal government that follows the principles of either a totalitarian or the fascist rule of law.

The definition of a totalitarian government: a government in which one political party or group maintains complete control and bans all others, ultimately authoritarian (*Webster's New Dictionary*, 1986). Islam only allows for a one party government.

The definition of fascism: a government by one-party dictatorship. It is a government who suppress opposition through the use of militant and or judicial authority. (Webster's New Dictionary, 1986). Islam, one party government, designed to suppress Christianity even at the hands of killing Christians.

One example of how Islam is the ultimate ruling authority is when it comes to education and free speech, one only need to read the life story of Mark A. Gabriel. In his book *"Jesus and Muhammad"* Mark Gabriel shares his story as a religious leader and an Islamic history instructor at Al-Azhar University, Cairo, Egypt. Gabriel tells how the Brotherhood would not allow his students to ask questions about the life of Muhammad. In so doing, he was persecuted (severely beaten) by the Brotherhood until he left the Muslim religion and became a Christian.

Here is the big problem for the people of Islam, being caught in the dilemma of a pseudo-ideology, that does not allow educational freedom. Yes, and this is so unfortunate for the population of Islam as they blindly become indoctrinated in a dogmatic belief. Why? It is the only way the Islam Brotherhood can maintain its power and domination. They enforce adherence to Sharia Law through police action, false facts of Muhammad, control of judicial courts, and control of voting rights. The Brotherhood understands if they allowed educational freedom and agency for the people, the faith-based population of Islam would sub-stantially decline to bring about the destruction of Islam. Without ques-tion Islam's god, Allah, and Islam's prophet Muhammad, are in total contradiction to the Bible, the Constitution, the principles of liberty, and the values of eternal life. As an example, Islam is the only religion that is killing people if they do not follow their religion. Is that the kind of a God the world needs?

When an individual follows the character of lying, disregarding the truth, and murdering, they have put themselves in the path as a child of Satan. Islam's Sleepers and Hearten may be decent people; however, they are irrelative because they refuse to stop the Brotherhood from fol-lowing satanic rules.

In closing, it is important to note how Jesus Christ gives the origin of ly-ing. He states:

> *"You are of your father the devil, and the desires of your father (Satan) you want to do. He was a murderer from the beginning, and does not stand in the truth, because there*

is no truth in him. When he speaks a lie, he speaks from his own resources, for he is a liar and the father of it."

- John 8:44

Question: When Islam openly lies, who is their father?

Wrapping UP

1. Muhammad shows signs of mental illness.
2. Muhammad is the only prophet to be illiterate.
3. Muhammad is the only prophet to lie openly.
4. He is the only prophet to murder people personally.
5. He is the only prophet to attack caravans to steal.
6. He is the only prophet to allow men to rape women.
7. He is the only prophet opens to slavery.
8. He is the only prophet to request assassination.
9. Islam lacks compassion for human rights.
10. Islam will not protect the rights of Christians or Jews.
11. Islam disregards the equal rights of women.
12. Islam falsifies the truth about the Quran.
13. The ruling of Taqiyya allows Muslims to lie.
14. Sharia Law is anti-American and anti-Constitutional.
15. Islam's world goal is to be the only existing government.
16. Allah does not show signs of being the true God of the Bible.
17. The Devil is the father of lies and murder.
18. The Quran does not allow for agency.

CHAPTER 5

—— ⸹ ——

Share the Truth

Blessed is the nation whose God is the LORD

PSALM 33:12

LOOKING BACK TO America's Founding Fathers through the 1950's, thinking about the values and principles Americans lived by during those times, without question today America is witnessing a deterioration of those values and principles.

Those were the times when people held on to the genuine "Spirit of America." Today that spirit, those morals, and ideals have been marginalized or replaced. Belief in the Constitution, personal liberties, the American family, and the devaluing of religious principles has reached the lowest spiritual ideals this country has ever witnessed.

Those who are truly grateful to live in America those who fully honor America, realize America is a covenant land guided by the influence of God, through the "Spirit of America."

Sad but true, today's generation may not agree with or even be aware what these concepts mean. They fail to understand what "Spirit of America" stands for and how deep its perception and capabilities are in offering freedom for humanity.

Over the last 65 years, the current generation has been indoctrinated with false social, moral, and intellectual values by those who desire to control America. Those wanting power and control over America are members of the Communist Party (One World Order), the American

Democratic Party, and/or Islam. What do these three have in common? What are their guiding principles? They are:

1. Rulers of Communist Religious Politics.
3. Anti-agency, anti-free will of man.
4. Anti-God. The God of this earth Jesus Christ.
5. Power Seekers.
6. The religion of Man over God.

Earlier it was asked: "What is happening? Where are we going as a nation? Just who are we today, and what has happened to our heritage as a nation?

As to what is happening, America is being reduced to a one-world order country. Just who are we today is answered when we understand we are being "Transformed" from a republican form of government to a social-communist form of government.

Moreover, to what is happening to our heritage, it is overrun by immigrants (legal and illegal) who do not understand and do not care about the "Spirit of America." These immigrants who have no desire to assimilate as actual American citizens, neither believing in and supporting the meaning of the Constitution.

For examples, we have cities that do not intend to follow the Constitution when becoming "sanctuary cities." People who illegally cross our borders become a public liability. Then we have citizens who live on entitlements instead of being a producer for society. Foreign flags are receiving respect over our American flag. Many of them are not willing to learn and speak the language of the country. Today 61 million households (21%) in America do not speak English in the home. (www.citylab.com/politics/2013/08/geography-americas-many.../6438/).

A second example is Islamics, who want to live in America but prefer to follow "Sharia Law' instead the U.S. Constitution.

A third example is elected leaders who fail to protect our borders, allowing immigrants to come freely into our country. They will not control our national debt or our national security. Some politicians are putting forth communist principles over American values.

Every one of these individuals is a disparaging American, who does not understand, care about, or is willing to strive to understand the distinct meaning of the "Spirit of America."

The above examples describe what it means when we say there is a "War on America." The biggest problem we face appears to be Americans who are so ill-informed about the "Spirit of America" that they are not willing to stand up to preserve their country. Remember what Benjamin Franklin said about what kind of a government they formed, "A republic, if you can keep it." How would Franklin respond to our form of government today?

Not only is there a "War on America", but there is also a "War on God". It is easy to understand how countries like Russia and China come across as anti-God. However, when viewing Islam and the Democratic Party, many will say that is so wrong. However, is it?

As for Islam, the individual they call Allah, is contrary to the principles of the Bible and the Constitution in numerous, crucial spiritual and political policies. His character and morals as Islam's god lack in multiple categories for showing love for humanity.

There is overwhelming proof of historical evidence to prove Jesus Christ as the only God of this world. As for Allah, there is absolutely no verification of his existence or godhood.

Christ personally walked the earth and performed many miracles. He spoke to and ordained many apostles and prophets and talked to thousands of people. It is recorded He even appointed Jeremiah as a prophet before the world was (Jeremiah 1:5). He gave His life for the world and was resurrected to overcome the bonds of death, that man could receive eternal life. Even the Quran states Christ will once again return to live on earth. Isaiah 45:23 informs the world every knee shall bow before Christ at the time of judgment.

Over 3,000 people have experienced and recorded "Near Death Experiences". Of those who have received personal knowledge of Jesus

Christ, when returning home, they offered testimony that Christ lives as a warm and most loving God. Those individuals who returned from the other side changed their lives to a more spiritual and higher standard of living.

Allah supposedly talked to one person known to be questionably mentally ill. He did not walk the earth, did not speak to or select other prophets. Allah left no organization or structure for the world to follow after the passing away of Muhammad. He failed to perform miracles. He failed to communicate with the people of the world. Allah made no sacrifice or commitment to benefit humanity.

The ethical standards of Islam authorize lying, rape, enslavement, and murder. Islam does not allow for the agency of man. In fact, if one chooses not to be of Islamic faith, Allah approves of killing that person. These ethics are in total contradiction to Christianity, to the Constitution, and to world freedom.

At times, the history of the Crusades is brought up for discussion. President Obama has mentioned the Crusades. Like an irrational fool, he fails to recognize Christians have moved on in a civil manner, Islam has not. Since that time in history Christians have not attempted to murder Muslims only to offer them freedom. However, Islam is not willing to move on; in fact, they are still living in the past as barbaric and primitive people. As an example:

"Nine of the 10 countries with the worst records for the persecution of Christians have populations that are at least 50 percent Muslim, according to the assessment of persecution in the Open Doors USA's World Watch List (WWL) 2015."

"Approximately 100 million Christians are persecuted worldwide, making them one of the most persecuted religious groups in the world," said an Open Doors statements announcing the report. "**Islamic extremism is the main source of persecution** in 40 of the 50 countries on the 2015 World Watch List." (Bold added).

(http://www.cnsnews.com/news/article/lauretta-brown/9-10-worst-countries-persecution-christians-have-50-or-greater-muslim).

"It is being reported Islamic is **exterminating Christians** in the Middle East." Believed within five years, there will no longer be Christians in any country of the Middle East." (Bold added).

(http://www.foxnews.com/world/2015/11/09/on-brink-christianity-facing-middle-east-purge).

"On the brink: Christianity facing Middle East purge within a decade, says group…The Christian population in Iraq has plummeted from 1.5 million in 2003 to current estimates of 275,000 and could be gone for good within five years, according to reports". (http://www.wsj.com/articles/exterminating-christians-in-the-middle-east-1440112782).

The Middle East is where Christianity began and because of the Muslim people they are on the brink of extermination, of genocide. Why is this happening? Islam is working for their god, Allah, whose design is to destroy/control all Christians. To completely erase Christianity and Jesus Christ from the earth as the Sleepers and Heartens just stand by doing nothing as they claim they are of peace.

Islam has not emotionally left the Crusade that took place from 1095 to 1291 A.D. The Crusades represent some of the most barbaric and dangerous periods. Christians have changed; it is Christian nations who are coming to the aid of Muslims. This is something Islam has never done in the entire history of Allah.

Islam has reverted to hateful, barbaric, and primitive people living 800 years behind the times of society. They are putting human beings in a cage and setting them on fire, cutting the throats of thousands of Christians, and selling off girls as sex slaves. They are also, calling for the destruction of Israel and America.

How is it that those who are the Sleepers and Hearten people of Islam justify sitting back doing nothing to help save the life of innocent human beings. Their inaction stands alone to falsify the claim that "Islam is a religion of peace".

As the claim of being a member of the human race, it is inexcusable to make the assertion Allah can be the god of this world. In the year 2000, B.C. Arabia worships Allah, as the pagan moon god. Today what is the actual position Allah holds? Who is he and where does he live? Other than the word of a psychologically ill man there is no proof of Allah's existence. Christians have recordings of 1,000's who have seen Him, Jesus Christ, and witness of His Godhood. This is something Islam can not replicate.

It is time for Islam to overcome their communist ideology. Time to understand who is the loving God, who loves all humanity.

It is unreasonable to believe there can be an existence of two Gods on this earth. It has to be either Jesus Christ or Allah. At this time, the culture clash between Islam, Christ, and America is alarming. Islam gives all serious thought of being an ideology, lacking in moral equivalency to the principles of freedom, of America, and of Christianity.

When a man takes the time to study the life and character of these men, Allah is so diminished by the deeds and love of Christ it is impossible to consider any God except for Jesus Christ, the creator of this world, the Son of God the Father.

DESTRUCTION WITHIN

History has shown, more often than not, nations are destroyed by enemies from within, rather than from foreign countries. That is happening to America today. Our own Democratic Party is destroying America's Constitution, American values, the family, and America's love of God.

As of this date, with Comrade Obama as president of the United States of America, the Democratic Party has reached its pinnacle towards transforming America from a republic to the underworld of the One World Order. Comrade Obama has advanced the Democratic Party to the state of an open War against God. Over the last 65 years, Democrats have actively been reconditioning America into a communist form of government. Many may say communism no, but perhaps socialism. Socialism is only the back door approach to introducing and establishing the long-term means of communism designed to take full control of the political uninformed voting people.

To further demonstrate how the Democratic Party has split away from God and country; let's review the voting policies and principles of Comrade President Obama and his Democratic Party in comparison to the Founding Fathers (FF), and Heavenly Father as follows:

Policies	Obama/Dems	F.F.	God
Entitlement programs	Yes	No	No
Illegal immigration	Yes	No	No
Tax supported abortion	Yes	No	No
Redistribution of money	Yes	No	No
Homosexual marriage	Yes	No	No
Unfettered transgender	Yes	No	No
Big Government	Yes	No	No
EPA property control	Yes	No	No
Removal of God-platform	Yes	No	No
Support of Islam	Yes	No	No
Support of Israel	No	Yes	Yes
1st Amendment rights	No	Yes	Yes
2nd Amendment rights	No	Yes	Yes
10th Amendment rights	No	Yes	Yes
DOMA	No	Yes	Yes
Exceptionalism	No	Yes	Yes
Fiscal Responsibility	No	Yes	Yes
Kates Law	No	Yes	Yes
World's strongest military	No	Yes	Yes

To some degree, just about everything God and our Founding Fathers would support the Democratic Party disregards. Why? Because to stand in support of God's principles, the original intent of the Constitution means they will lose their power and control over America.

According to Alex Griswold of Mediait.com (11/03/2015)

here is an example of how far Obama and the Democratic Party have reached: Obama's Department of Education is forcing schools to allow unfettered transgender access to showers. Girls will be required to take a shower in the presence of naked boys. OK, Comrade Obama when will the daughters or wife of the Obama family be in those showers? Plus, consider his actions of an unfettered woman military. Not only are these acts morally wrong they are evil, and also satanic.

On June 26, 2015, four of the Supreme Court's liberals joined Justice Anthony Kennedy in discovering a new **unwritten right** to same-sex marriage in the U.S. Many were thrilled at this decision including the White House as Comrade President Obama ordered the White House to light up as a rainbow. Why? As a communist, he is supporting goals #26 and #40 to assist in destroying marriage and the family.

Others were equally happy with this decision, "among them, Communist Party USA and its publication, People's World—successor to the Soviet-funded and directed Daily Worker—were thrilled with what Anthony Kennedy and friends had done.

"For a communist, this was a stunning victory, the securing of a long-elusive effort to vanquish the fixed marriage model set forth long ago by nature and our Creator. Indeed, if you thought the White House seemed eager to hoist the rainbow colors, you should have seen the American Communist Party." (The Dailey Signal Morning Bell, Oct. 20, 2015, How the Left Has Sabotaged Marriage and Family). (Underlining added).

Why are the Democrats pushing these immoral acts? Answer: to support the goals of the Communist movement, to gain power, to break down the family by aligning with the following:

1. Get control of the schools #17
2. Continue discrediting American culture #22
3. Eliminate all laws governing obscenity #23
4. Break down cultural standards of morality #25
5. Present homosexuality #26
6. Support any socialist movement #32
7. Discredit the family as an institution #40

8. Emphasize the need to raise children away from the negative influence of parents #41

Again the Democratic Party is mandating their communist position when placing the illegal criminal immigrants' liberties over the welfare of American citizens, and refusing to pass Kates Law to protect Americans from violent people.

CREATION OF COMMUNISM

Why Communism and where did it originate? Possibly the first recording of Communism took place in the Bible telling of Cain killing (influenced by Satan) Able to take control his property. Islam started in the year 610 A.D. Lenin officially organized Communism in 1919.

However, there are signs it began even before the creation of the world. According to Revelations 12:7-10 (KJV)

[7] "And there was war in heaven: Michael and his angels fought against the dragon; and the dragon fought and his angels,

[8] And prevailed not; neither was their place found any more in heaven.

[9] And the great dragon was cast out, that old serpent, called the Devil, and Satan, which deceiveth the whole world: **he was cast out into the earth, and his angels were cast out with him.**

[10] And I heard a loud voice saying in heaven, Now is come salvation, and strength, and the kingdom of our God, and the **power of his Christ**: for the accuser of our brethren is cast down, which accused them before our God day and night." (Bold added)

The war that took place in the heavens was not a military war but a war of ideas, a religious, political war. A war where Satan is against God the Father and His Son Jesus Christ. Satan wants control over those in heaven, to control their agency. However, Christ's purpose was to design agency as the principle of humanity. The **cast-down Satan** still wants to control the world. Heaven's war is still in existence today here on this earth. Of the two forms of political religions in heaven, one is to follow

Jesus Christ, freedom of will, and the other is designed to adhere to the principles of Satan, Communism. On earth today, there is Christianity and Jesus Christ, versus Communism and Satan.

One's actions on earth will determine their place of existence in the next life. Each person has choices to make, either freedom of agency or communism to follow the leaders of communism (One World Order, Democratic Party, and Islam). Because of free will, it is the right of each citizen to choose what way of life to live by in America for this coming election. America and her citizens' futures depend on what voting choices they make.

SPIRIT OF AMERICA

The words "Spirit of America" have often been said or used by individuals to express their feeling and love for their country. These words are not placed together in the dictionary nor is there a standard written definition for its genuine meaning. That is because there is a deep and real significance and purpose of those words. There are two parts to this phase, Spirit, and America.

SPIRIT: The word Spirit as defined means: "the life principles regarded as inherent in the breath of or as infused by a deity." (Webster's New World Dictionary, 1984, p. 1293).

When describing America, the word deity refers to God, Jesus Christ. After receiving persecution by governments, being forced to follow a certain creed, Pilgrims journeyed to the new world, for the first time being able to use their agency to worship according to the ways of their heart.

Overwhelmingly their hearts, from the very beginning, were set to follow the deity of Jesus Christ as their life principles. When studying early American history, it becomes self-evident that Jesus Christ is the only deity American's came to the western continent to worship. It had nothing to do with Judaism, Islam, or any other religion, plain and simple only Jesus Christ.

In regards to Christ and the definition of "life principles," this tells the world America is to follow the principles, laws, and life teachings of Jesus Christ and no other form of faith.

Those life principles are:

"Jesus said unto him, Thou shalt love the Lord thy God with all thy heart, and with all thy soul, and with all thy mind.

38 This is the first and great commandment.

39 And the second is like unto it, Thou shalt love thy neighbour as thyself.

40 On these two commandments hang all the law and the prophets." (Matthew 22:36-40).

When following the Laws, the Ten Commandments, and their principles, fusing them together, they become the breath of life fulfilling America's way of living. Combined together, they become the "Spirit of America".

NOTE: America has a president who is not able to uphold America as an Exceptional Nation, unable to feel the "Spirit of America." Communism will never support these American Mottos.

AMERICA: Why America? A short answer is as follows; during the time of Adam the world was of one land. After the flood, the world was divided into geographic areas. The Western Hemisphere was, by strategy, separated from other continents. Why? To prepare America's future to be a land of freedom.

The time span of this earth comprises of seven dispensations, seven periods of man's preparation before the Millenium, Christ's returning to govern a free world.

After Christ's resurrection, and after the apostles were taken from the earth, the Religious Political principles of Christianity were forced to take cover due to the controlling government leaders and misguided Religious organizations who would not allow a man to live by free agency. The man was either persecuted, restricted in their faith, or forced to follow a government-approved church.

Forced political religion was the fundamental reason for the War in Heaven, Satan's plan against the eternal principles of God, fighting for the control of man's agency (Communism). However, God's plan does not force anyone into Heaven. It comes about by agency, the free will of man. That is why there is a time and purpose of Judgement, for a man to decide his destiny based on how he is willing to make use of his free agency while on earth.

During the era of the 15th century, there was no government upon the earth allowing free agency. In preparations for the coming of Christ, the spirit called Columbus to open the seas to the New World. Next, many believers of Christ were lead to the New World.

As the New World became settled, inspired men fought for freedom and created the world's first free republican Constitution for the agency of man under the guiding hand and assistance of God.

Under God's direction, America is called upon as His people to safe-guard the free will of man in planning for the Millennium and His return. America's reason and purpose for its design are to uphold the world in opening the way for Jesus Christ. Here lies the precise reason God created America as His Christian Nation.

Satan does not want Christ to open up the Millennium. It is Satan's goal to overshadow the world not to recognize Jesus Christ when He returns. That is the ultimate purpose of Communism. To destroy Christianity, families, and the Constitution, to terminate the love of Christ, Allah's followers to extinguish Christians, Communism against Christianity.

As a closing **definition** of *"The Spirit of America," written as "The inherent breath of deity, Jesus Christ" directed by the hand of Christ, to defend man's eternal agency, man's liberty."*

Now, citizens know the "rest of the story" as why today we are facing a War on America, a War on God."

America; is there a need for any more evidence of whom the Democratic Party Leadership represents? What is their underlying motive for America? When voting Democrats step into the voting booth, this coming election will they continue to vote for Communism? What kind of America do voters want for this generation? What will be told when bowing the knee before Christ about moral decisions made at the voting booth? This country is designed to belong to the people. In the upcoming election, what kind of a nation will the people want? Will we have a democratic/communist form of government or a Republic form of government?

America where do YOU stand? What actions or response should Americans make in the upcoming election?

During the American Civil War, both the South and the North believed they were correct to fight for their political rights and that God was on their side. One was for the right to control slavery and the other the right to free men from slavery. The Democrats want us to believe they are right in leading us to become a communist form of government. That is the position America will be voting for when stepping into the voting booth next November. Democrats will vote for slavery, others will be voting for freedom. Abraham Lincoln responded to those during the Civil War, believing God was on their side when saying; "It is not my concerns that God is on my side, it is my greatest concern to be on God's side for He is always right."

Today, what is required of us to bring America back to God's side?

1. **Renewing our trust in God:** Our Founding Fathers put their trust in God to win over England and to form a perfect union when creating the Constitution.

    During the Constitutional Convention, the Founders called upon God in prayer for guidance. George Washington prayed humbly for God's sustaining assistance at Valley Forge. James Madison stated, *"It is impossible for the man of pious reflection not to perceive in it [the Constitution] a finger of that Almighty hand which has been so frequently and signally*

117

extended to our relief in the critical stages of the revolution." Even the Supreme Court on February 29, 1892, "declared (in *Holy Trinity v. United States*) that the historical record of America overwhelmingly demonstrated that the United States *"... is a Christian nation."*

America's originating roots lay in the footprints of God. If one does not want to believe in God that is within their rights, however, that does not disregard the fact we are His covenant nation.

2. ***Return to the original intent of the Constitution:*** A *federal* government to govern only a *federation* of states. The essential duties of the federal government are:
   A. To ensure the states function well between themselves, such as with interstate commerce and public acts.
   B. To provide for the common defense.
   C. Oversee proper relationships with foreign countries.
   D. All other duties are the responsibilities of the states, the local governments or the people.

3. ***Fortify the First, Second, and Tenth Amendments.*** Guarding our God-given rights to self-protection, freedom of speech, and God-given right to freedom of religion. Return to a federation of States over Communism.

4. ***Support the Family as the keystone in building our Nation.*** Encourage rules of responsibility and virtue. Provide parent support in raising the family. Build upon family principles and values.

5. ***Promote True American Form of Government:*** based on Federalism, States Rights, **Knowledge of Liberty, Justice, Citizenship, and Patriotism.**

6. ***Teach the correct principles of our history.*** Our Founding Fathers and the religious principles as the foundation of this country.

7. ***Defend against all Religious Political acts that counter the original principles of the Constitution.*** Courts to uphold the Founding Fathers intent of our Constitution. Outside sources not to be considered legal laws of the land (U.N. and Sharia Laws).

8. ***Return education to the hands of the parents.*** Allow for religious expression combined with Constitutional instructions. Teach the meaning of Exceptionalism.

   "[T]he only foundation for a useful education in a **republic is to be an aid in religion**. Without this, there can be no virtue, and without virtue there can be no liberty, and liberty is the object and life of all republican governments. Without religion, I believe that learning does real mischief to the morals and principles of mankind". (Benjamin Rush signer of the Constitution) (Bold added).

   "Whereas true religion and good morals are the only solid foundations of public liberty and happiness . . . it is hereby earnestly recommended to the several States to take the most effectual measures for the encouragement thereof." (Continental Congress, 1778, Benjamin Franklin).

9. ***Citizenship***. Required to follow the proper rules for application. One parent required to be a citizen for a child to become a citizen.

10. ***Immigration:*** Based on needs of the country. Those applying must speak English, pass health and criminal background checks. Not eligible for tax-supported government programs. Not available to vote. If states provide forms of identification, they must indicate the holder is a visitor, not a registered voter.

11. ***English:*** Recognized as the official language of the country. Currently, there are over 120 different languages spoken in America. It is essential for all citizens to be capable of communicating with each other to build national unity, strengthen America, and create pride to be an American.

12. ***Balanced Budget:*** Reduce our national debt. Require a balanced budget amendment.

AMERICA 1ˢᵗ

"When standing up to do what is right, one man will become a majority."

Attributed to Jackson by Robert F. Kennedy

As Edmond Burke tells us, for evil to exist, good men only need to do nothing. Our Founding Fathers were men not willing to allow evil to exist. They pledged their lives, their fortunes, and their sacred honor for an unheard of, an undefined America, never fearing the consequences.

One man can become a majority. However, when good citizens join one man, America will return once again to "we the people". If you would like to be that one person joined by good citizens to overcome evil, please envision working with America 1ˢᵗ at **www.america1st.us.**

Consider joining America 1ˢᵗ, working to repair the wrong taking place in our country, bring back America to the dedicated hard working people. We are reaching a critical time in history, for the survival of America, for good citizens to work together. We must unquestionably make sure the needs of America, American values, principles, and family come first to overthrow Communist goals. Let's transform America back to America, AMERICA 1ˢᵗ.

WRAPPING UP

1. Today, we are failing to understand what the "Spirit of America" represents.
2. Over the last 65 years, the current generation has been indoctrinated with false social, moral, and intellectual values.
3. The moral and ethics of Islam are in total contradiction to Christianity, to the Constitution, and to world freedom.
4. History has shown, more often than not, nations are destroyed by enemies from within.
5. Communism will never support America's Mottos of Exceptionalism and the "Spirit of America".

6. Unfettered sex-gender: these acts (schools and military) are morally wrong, it is evil and satanic.
7. Democratic Party has split away from God and country.
8. "The Spirit of America": The inherent breath of deity, to defend man's eternal agency, man's liberty.
9. It is impossible for there to be two Gods on this earth. God has to be either Jesus Christ or Allah.
10. When a man takes the time to study the life and character of Christ, Allah is diminished by the deeds and love of Christ.
11. The reason and purpose for the creation of America is to safeguard the world in opening the way for Jesus Christ.
12. America called upon as people of Christ to defend the free will of man in preparation for the Millenium and His return.
13. One man can become a majority.
14. Let's transform America back to America. AMERICA 1ST.

DEAR READER,

If you have a desire in "Standing up and preserving America", to restore the true "Spirit Of America," please share this book with others then go to www.america1st.us. The very existence of this nation will depend upon your desire to be that "One Man" to be the majority.

Sincerely,
Philip Clark